We Danced All Night

We Danced All Night

My Life Behind the Scenes
with Alan Jay Lerner

DORIS SHAPIRO

WILLIAM MORROW AND COMPANY, INC.
New York

Grateful acknowledgment is made for use of lyrics from:

"Camelot." Words by Alan Jay Lerner, music by Frederick Loewe. Copyright ©
1960 (renewed). All rights administered by WB Music Corp. All rights reserved.
Used by permission.

"Melinda" from *On a Clear Day You Can See Forever.* Words by Alan Jay Lerner,
music by Burton Lane. Copyright © 1965 by Alan Jay Lerner and Burton Lane.
Chappell and Company owner of publication and allied rights. International
copyright secured. All rights reserved.

Library of Congress Cataloging-in-Publication Data

Shapiro, Doris.
   We danced all night: my life behind the scenes with Alan Jay Lerner /
   Doris Shapiro.
      p.   cm.
   ISBN 0-688-08937-2
   1. Lerner, Alan Jay, 1918–1986.   2. Librettists—United States—
Biography.   I. Title.
ML423.L3S5   1990
782.1'4'092—dc20
   [B]   89-36522
                                                                CIP

Printed in the United States of America

FIRST EDITION

1 2 3 4 5 6 7 8 9 10

BOOK DESIGN BY PAUL CHEVANNES

My most affectionate thanks to Bud (Stone) Widney for coaxing my memory of parts of our lives in numerous phone conversations.

And to Herman Levin, who reminded me that the top price for a ticket to *My Fair Lady* was $6.05.

We Danced All Night

Prologue

One day in 1988 I ran into an acquaintance from the 1950's. She used to be secretary to Vincent Donehue, a man who directed Broadway musicals that starred Mary Martin.

I remembered she had married a businessman named Irwin, and after a while I didn't hear of her anymore.

As we stood on the corner, catching up on our lives, she said to me, "The other day Irwin said he was sorry."

"For what?"

"For making me quit my job."

I had to control the urge to laugh.

"But, Rosalind, that was thirty years ago!"

To my amazement, I saw she was carrying a grudge since the 1950's against her husband, which she produced now with two little bitter shakes of the head.

"When we were first married and Vincent would call me at eight o'clock at night, Irwin said, 'Why is he calling you at home at this hour?' And when I had my bags packed and was walking to the door to go on the road with a show, he locked me in the house!"

This time I laughed out loud.

She said nostalgically, "But it was such a *fun* job. Well, *you* know. Your husband didn't stop *you*."

"No, he didn't," I said, realizing that she had been barely brushed by the outside layers of the experience. I left her unenlightened, but as we parted and I walked away, I thought: Those fun jobs, those thrillers, if you came to them with the right ingredients, could turn from fun to obsession. And if taken to their extreme, could end in extermination.

Where had my fun ended and the obsession begun? At what point should I have unpacked my bags?

I

The whole long fun-filled, life-threatening story started inno-
cently enough one summer morning in 1952, when I was
summoned to Lillie Messinger's Frank Lloyd Wright house in
Beverly Hills. Three years out of UCLA, lingering too long
at home, and at the moment not in love, I was vaguely at loose
ends.

I swung my car up to the curb on the palmy, sun-dappled
street and got out. The only sound in the neighborhood came
from my heels clacking up the walk.

Marlene Dietrich, looking fragile and parched without
makeup, answered the door in a robe. I didn't know she was
in town or that she was so small.

Embarrassed for her exposure at the open door, I said, "Forgive me, I'm here to see Lillie." She gave me one of her famous
penetrating but distant looks, with barely parted lips. "I can
find my way," I said apologetically.

She stood back for me to enter and then wafted off into the
depths of the house. I went past the indoor waterfall, silent
now, to the wood-paneled den that someone earlier had added.

Lillie came toward me, beaming, as if I were a prize. She
always started a visit by telling me I never looked more beautiful.

"Dotty, dear!" (My pet name, used by people close to me.)

"You get to look more and more like Ava Gardner, doesn't she, Alex?"

Lillie was a nurturer; she always sounded proud of you.

"That's our Dotty," Alex said, with some gaiety.

In his fifties in a navy blue blazer with a silk scarf tied around his throat, he was tall, straight, and tan, though a little puffy in the face.

Lillie, small, slightly plump, was colorful in her pastel California knits, with sensible white shoes and wavy hair reddish blond from her hairdresser.

They were Prince and Princess Alexis Thurn-Taxis.

Letting me know this was not a casual visit, Alex said to their two German shepherds, which jumped to his side, "Come on, boys," and to Lillie, "I'll go pick up Marlene's gown while you girls talk."

When there were no more B movies being made, Alex had retired from directing them, and from then on it was Lillie who had kept the luxury liner afloat financially, although Alex protected her from all else. They called her Scheherezade at Metro-Goldwyn-Mayer because although she suffered stage fright, she could face a roomful of producers and directors and tell a story that she had found so enticing that they would want to put it on film. Louis B. Mayer would say to her, even once from a hospital bed, "Do you like it, Lillie?"

"Yes, Mr. Mayer."

"Buy it, Lillie."

And it would be *Easter Parade* or something else big.

But with the death of Louis B. Mayer and the collapse of the big studios, Lillie fell from privilege to the supplicant role of agent, which was when I met and worked for her in Johnny Maschio's talent agency. Johnny introduced girls to oilmen from Texas on the side and would be picked up now and then by a big black car to go to an undisclosed place to talk with

Howard Hughes. Corruption this raw made Lillie weep at her desk sometimes, and that's how we became friends.

Lillie and Alex were both real and Hollywood royalty; they went to Lady Mendl's parties, and Lillie had her hair done at Elizabeth Arden's. But they were the poorest of their set, and the house was up for sale.

Lillie was now agent only for her cherished Alan Jay Lerner. Ever since she had fallen in love with his script and lyrics for *Brigadoon*, she had involved herself in every detail of his career and personal life.

As we sat on the down sofa, surrounded by pieces of silver and antiques and signed photographs of much of Hollywood, Lillie inclined her wavy head toward me and, with an intimate smile, said, "I want to tell you, Alan Lerner is here from New York."

The way she drawled her words made what she said seem important. Merely speaking his name brought a glow to her.

"He's come out to do some writing."

She sat back, crossed her manicured hands, and paused. Then, looking into my eyes earnestly, she announced, "I'd like you to go meet him today and help him for the next two weeks."

Lillie's transparency made me smile. An introduction arranged by her was never random and usually had consequences. I knew at once the scenario was that if he liked me, I could end up moving to New York. I had watched her match people: stars and writers to producers and directors. Each union was a masterpiece. Even in her retirement it was her pride that Hollywood people still came for her advice.

But Alan Jay Lerner was Lillie's most prized possession. He was her genius. And as I glanced up at his familiar picture on her mantel, I felt that I was always supposed to meet and work for him.

Lillie knew I already had my own genius. He was my brother, Howard; bigger than life, ruddy, with noble eyebrows and a dusky radiance in his eyes; moral, moody, wildly funny, brilliant. I grew up with him and the lifelong smell of oil paints and turpentine. I had sat contentedly for hours in Howard's studio, as he draped me clumsily with fabric and painted me, and I never for a moment resented being introduced at parties as Howard Warshaw's sister. In my purse was a newspaper review of Howard's latest exhibit: "Passion and intellect mingle in the powerful art of Howard Warshaw." "We believe," he said to his students, "that inert matter, earth materials, charcoal dust moving across paper, raw umber moving across linen can become possessed by the spirit of man."

So I had already learned to idolize, as Lillie did, and I knew the rules of hero worship.

"I entrust you to Alan with a free heart," Lillie was saying, preparing me for the sacred ritual that she meant to take place.

I had mixed feelings of excitement, yes, but also amusement and resistance at the prospect of meeting Alan Jay Lerner. Amusement because I had already helped put him through Harvard. I had spent my eighteenth year, after high school, working behind a counter selling $3.98 blouses and sweaters six days a week in one of his father's many Lerner Shops. These shops operated on the principles of terror and slavery. There was always someone above watching you. When the executives paid a surprise visit, it was the tyrannical manager's turn to cringe. Even I got to watch someone: the stock clerk. I worked with a rather rough, high-spirited bunch of women who called me "bedroom eyes" and laughed when I blushed. I brought home $18 a week and didn't perceive in my teenage years that some women got caught in this sort of job forever. I slipped out of it and into college, shed the experience without a scar.

Resistance to meeting him because although I had been

exposed to Hollywood glamour, I was shy; also, I knew nothing about the New York musical theater, and I didn't really care. I could never remember who wrote the words and who wrote the music, and I had never seen Lerner and Loewe's *Brigadoon* or *Paint Your Wagon*. I had an ignorant indifference to Broadway musicals. Our crowd was a mix of musicians, would-be writers, painters, and dancers, and I had been brought up on Mozart, Rubinstein, and Heifetz.

My lively and emotional family was descended from rural Russian Jews, although they never behaved like refugees. It was my brother, Howard, who rose and took us with him. By the late forties his work was shown in three galleries: the sociable Little Gallery, hosted engagingly by Vincent Price and his buddy from New York stage days George Macready; Vera Stravinsky's gallery, on La Cienega Boulevard; and, for yearly trips, the prestigious Julian Levy Gallery on Fifty-seventh Street in New York.

As I drove away from Lillie's that day, I was aware I had few defenses against enchantment—part of my nature—but I didn't think I'd need any. The Alan Lerner I had seen yesterday on Rodeo Drive, stepping out of the depths of a limousine, was a young peacock, who tossed his head feudally to the chauffeur before disappearing into a shop. I didn't switch geniuses easily.

The bougainvillaea and oleander were blooming in the sun and waving in the breeze that afternoon as I walked up the path of the Bel Air Hotel and knocked on the bungalow door.

"Come!"

Alan Jay Lerner sat in a big chair, with his bare feet pulled up and a script on his knees. In smooth cream-colored pants and a slim yellow turtleneck, from which his narrow, youthful chin emerged cleanly, he looked ready to go for a drive in a convertible on the Riviera with Ingrid Bergman. He threw me a friendly, mock SOS glance, as his daughter Liza tried to crawl into his lap. Through the open bedroom door I saw his wife, Nancy, unpacking a trunk with the help of a hotel maid.

"You're about to save my life," he said cheerfully, casting his handsome, slightly careworn gaze on me, and from the full ripeness of his domesticity, he smiled the sweetest smile that ever came to rest on a martyr's lips. "I'm on a deadline."

He took Liza on his lap.

"Sit down."

Relief! I had him all wrong. He wasn't at all the fancy show-off I thought I saw yesterday. He was a charmer. I felt wrapped in his invisible embrace, as though he had known me all his life and mine and treasured the moment with me, only me. Years later I decided the explanation for this talent; it was so simple one tended to overlook it: Alan was genuinely sincere for the full length of each encounter.

"The thing is," he said, "I've got to lick this scene."

I sat down in the deep, soft chair opposite him and crossed my legs. And I stayed for the next fourteen years.

Alan had come out from New York to write some scenes for the movie of *Brigadoon*, while his wife, Nancy Olson, who had starred in *Sunset Boulevard*, was working in a film. She was racing her pregnancy, which caught up with her the night shooting finished, and her stomach suddenly swelled, with Jennifer inside.

As the two weeks went by, Alan's talent began to work on me. He actually wrote out loud; I would take the dialogue down in shorthand, read it back to him, then type it up. He would deliver a line and look at me expectantly, and I marveled, sometimes to him, at how he got from one moment in the script to the next. He could be going along and, with one line, move the whole action of the piece a degree forward.

Sometimes he would go to the little white hotel piano and

play and sing for me. The song that haunted me was "Another Autumn" from *Paint Your Wagon,* and this revealed the presence of that other artist, the composer, Frederick Loewe, the man next to Alan at the piano in the photograph on Lillie's mantel. His voice was my first emotional experience of the team of Lerner and Loewe.

One afternoon after work, toward the end of the two weeks, my old blue Plymouth wouldn't start. I tried and tried. Giving up, I went back, embarrassed, and knocked on the bungalow door. Alan Lerner answered.

"I'm terribly sorry, but my battery's dead. Could I make a call?"

"Don't worry," he said. "I'll see to it. Come on, I'll drive you home."

I saw that here was a take-charge man with resources and wealth.

When I got to know him better, I realized I had come back at a moment in the late afternoon when he was alone and at loose ends. He welcomed the diversion.

I lived only ten minutes away in Beverly Hills. Careening good-naturedly down the long hill from Sunset Boulevard, I got the feeling that life with Alan was full of small perils, little dramas that amused rather than threatened. As the car bumped over something in the road, Alan said, "Was that somebody?"

"Not anybody we know," I said.

We reached Wilshire Boulevard. "One block east of Doheny, and one block and five houses south," I said.

He pulled up in his flashy little convertible to our Spanish house with the arches and patio and grilled living-room window, similar to the rest of the houses on the street.

"Thank you so very much," I said.

He made no move to go.

I didn't know what to do. "Would you like to come in for a drink?" I said hesitantly.

"Sure."

As I got to know Alan in later years, I realized it was his natural storyteller's curiosity that brought him through my parents' door that day.

My mother and father were used to my bringing home all sorts of people. They would behave with the awed pleasure they showed when Howard brought home Vincent Price or Henry Miller.

My dad sat comfortably, having his bourbon on the rocks, listening to his latest record, the overture to *La Forza del Destino,* and reading the desert real estate section of the newspaper. My mother, discarding her apron held out her hand with veiled eyes and a shy, flirty smile.

"Mr. Lerner," she said. It was she who was the original hero worshiper. "Do sit down."

Alan sat at the edge of the long, cushy couch and refused a drink. I only wanted my father, an old Lerner Shop production manager, to resist telling Alan he had known his famous sports-fishing, philanthropic uncle Mike Lerner.

Alan paid no attention to Howard's pictures on the wall. Later I learned he preferred paintings of sailboats with flags waving at Nice by Dufy to Howard's more elemental and intellectual paintings.

When, in the midst of talking about California and New York, Alan, looking at my parents as though he needed permission—all an act—in a carefree way, as if he were proposing a jaunt to the ice-cream parlor, said, "Would you like to come back to New York and work for me?" I was a goner.

A little background here. New York was no stranger to me. It was the scene of my happy childhood, until at the age of sixteen, my father's small business collapsed and I was torn out of Music and Art High School to drive with my parents across

the country, following family and friends to the West Coast.
I had been back three or four times.

In those early poor days I missed the city streets and dark
winter afternoons, just as the refugees we met from the war in
Europe must have missed their capital cities.

To this day the sight of a poinsettia plant reminds me of the
three tall, scrawny ones leaning against the yellowish stucco of
the two-story apartment house on the forlorn flat street of that
name where we first landed in California.

Most of all, I missed my black-haired Russian piano teacher,
Nina Grossavitch, who looked like Dolores Del Rio. The Vas-
sidy Zavadsky piano studio had been the center of my life.
Though my dear mother found me another piano teacher in
California as soon as things got better, without Nina I never
again practiced four hours every afternoon. To this day I can
still play Chopin's "Revolutionary Etude," but that's all.

But because my brother, Howard, was there with us, he
turned everything to jokes—for me at any rate. We would
stretch out on parallel beds that came out of walls and play
word games, or he would draw faces of imaginary offspring
that bizarre couplings would produce—for example, Joseph
Stalin and Fanny Brice or Eleanor Roosevelt and Albert Ein-
stein.

Howard had the biggest love affair with life of anybody I
knew. A mere bath was a lavish, thunderous affair, with the
sound of the hot-water faucet pouring out intermittently to
replenish the tub, and his tremolo voice sending out shaky
melodies from Beethoven's Fifth Symphony or "People Will
Say We're in Love."

He could be dismaying. One night at dinner he punched his
fist through the wall as my father said one time too often,
"Why don't you paint pleasant pictures?"

And then there was the night sometime later, when our

family fortunes had improved and we each had our own room. Howard and I were by ourselves, he in his room painting and I in the living room with a new recording of *Tristan and Isolde*, ten sides on the 33 rpm disks. I found the climactic side, "The Love Death," and I played it about five times when suddenly Howard's door opened, and with a suppressed, edited fury, he said, "Dotty, if you play that one more time, I'm going to crack your head open."

By now Howard had begun his great teaching career. He sometimes let me into his intellectual circles, so I met Aldous Huxley, Christopher Isherwood, Igor Stravinsky, Henry Miller, and some assorted Hollywood people at parties. I had only to offer my sweetest smile, say, "How do you do?" and listen to develop a little glamour as Howard's lovely sister.

My life from the age of sixteen was one romantic quest after another. I got my romantic predilections as a direct shot into the umbilical cord from my charming mother.

When George Macready, that theater-wise Hollywood actor, said to her one night at our house, in his clipped, resonant New England voice, "If I were twenty years younger, I could have a crush on your daughter," she responded with a romantic tilt of her head and a wistful little twist of her lips, "If I were my daughter, I could have a crush on you."

She was giving me to him and taking him away from me at the same time!

But marriage! That was my mother's goal. Marriage, the ultimate, transcendental rescue by the superbeing who would appear and possess and release all the joy. Her elaborately tactful denials of alarm over my singlehood only increased the pressure. Did she think I didn't know it? It was time to get away.

Meanwhile, I was coming to the end of the year my parents had offered me to stay home and write, following the publication of my first and last short story. Though I worked hard and had piles of typewritten pages, I could make nothing happen on the pages the way Alan Lerner could, and I was tired of trying.

But here was Alan Jay Lerner inviting me to be part of the great Broadway musical at its best. I could sit back and watch *him* write.

I exchanged glances with my mother.

"Oh." She barely breathed with delight. At least one of us was going to have an adventure.

"Yes," I said.

"How soon can you pack and come?" He smiled and got up to go.

In those days a hundred dollars seemed enough money to buy anything I might want, even three pairs of Chanel shoes from a Madison Avenue shop.

Alan was going to pay me that much every week. I felt absolutely protected.

My grasp of economics extended only to the common knowledge that I should allow one quarter of my income for rent. All the rest was mine to spend.

Within a day in New York I had found an apartment up a flight of carpeted stairs in a brownstone house, opposite the Lever Brothers building, off Park Avenue on Fifty-third Street. It cost seventy-five dollars a month—I was rich—it was one large, high room with a fireplace, a terrace I had to climb out of the window to get to, and it was surrounded by the great walls of the Tennis and Racquet Club and at that time the tower of CBS. There was a strange lovely fragrance within the woodwork. Something harmonious was going on in my life.

A few days later Bud Widney came to pick me up and drive me in the car to Alan's house in the country, where I would sometimes work.

* * *

I opened the door on a blond young Californian dressed for the country, who, with his sparkling blue eyes, looked ready to spread out his arms and sing to a girl in the glen in *Briga- doon*. He rolled on his heels when he walked, giving a mellow impression.

"I'm here to show you the way," he said, smiling. "Nice place." He ambled over to the window and looked out. "How'd you get it together so fast?"

Bud had known Alan's wife, Nancy, in their UCLA days, and that's how he met and came to work for Alan. I soon found out that at that time he was often the one who would greet Alan or Lillie Messinger at the airport and carry their suitcases. I watched him become Alan's man for all seasons with casting, crew, the director, designer, and all the artists, and in five years he would bring Alan the idea to do *Camelot*. Ultimately he became an unofficial silent collaborator on script and direction. As he grew more and more important to Alan, he added a reddish beard and took to a pipe. Alan had trouble finding a title for him. He was never satisfied with the one he finally picked: Production Supervisor.

On the way to the country on that late-summer day in 1952, as we crossed over the shining Hudson River on the George Washington Bridge, my new job seemed more of a lark than a duty. Bud and I were two Californians. By the time we pulled up to the house, we discovered that both our mothers were Christian Scientists, only his mother was a Christian Christian Scientist and mine was a Jewish one. His mother was the real thing. She actually withheld medical treatment, whereas mine was only an aspirer, who loved the dramatic testimonials of cures that people would declare in church on Sundays and did her daily lessons, though she still filled my childhood with dentist's visits, shots, medicine. We arrived at the house laughing.

Alan had a 250-year-old farmhouse, painted white and blue,

with many miniature rooms, in the rolling hills and woods of Rockland County. After that first trip I would often pick up the red Oldsmobile at the garage and drive out on clear fall days with the top down. We would hike up the path and across the country road to his studio, another little house. Someone would bring sandwiches on trays. It was often three in the morning when I returned to the city, and in those days, either of my youth or the youth of our times I felt perfectly safe and private driving back to town at that hour.

Frederick Loewe lived up the road in Katonah. I don't remember exactly when I met him, but ever since I'd seen the picture of him with Alan at the piano on Lillie's mantel and heard Alan play his music, I felt I'd always known him.

Fritz was a familiar Old World gallant, like Alan, not tall, agile, very appealing, with the glint of wit in his eyes. Older than Alan, he was a gift from Germany, not yet a rich man, a European who had the uncanny ear for composing music in any idiom: He could create a musical Scotland for *Brigadoon*, re-create the American gold rush era in *Paint Your Wagon*, and conjure up England in *My Fair Lady* and *Camelot*, turning the solid classical European background of his childhood into the unmistakable romantic, sophisticated sound of the great Broadway theater. The first time he came to Alan's house, I could see in his fond eyes that he treasured Alan.

Later on I found out that some people found Fritz outrageous. Judith Anderson, neighbor and friend of my brother in Santa Barbara, met him at a party once.

"He brags," she said to me haughtily, with her mouth turning down.

To me, Fritz's bragging was the tiniest part of him. He had plenty to brag about, but he mostly did so about his sexual prowess. Sometimes he got a response that puzzled him. At a party, after Judy Garland sang, he went up to her and said magnanimously, "Judy, I've been laid twice today, but this one was the best of all." She gave him an icy stare and walked away.

Lerner and Loewe weren't working together at this time. Alan, in one of his unfaithful forays with another composer, was writing *Li'l Abner*, a show inspired by the Al Capp comic strip, with Arthur Schwartz, a very sweet man. I would sit with Alan in the little country studio and wait patiently with my clipboard on my lap for the words, but I could soon tell he didn't have his heart in it.

Nevertheless, in anticipation of production, we moved into a no-nonsense office in a business building on Madison Avenue in the Forties, provided by Herman Levin, the producer of *Li'l Abner*. In later years we would have more glamorous and clamorous offices, and I would spend less and less time in them.

Bud and I were the only staff Alan had at that time. When I wasn't at the country house, I'd go to the office from about ten to five. Production was waiting for more script and score, and it was too soon for casting.

The job was turning out to be dullish. Gradually I was being inducted into the intricacies of Alan's life: his children, his tailors, his first wife, his mother, his doctors. I was waiting for a show to materialize. Instead, sometimes Alan would swoop into the office from the country and take me with him on one of his shopping sprees, or to the barber, or the dentist. I began to travel around town with him, in those days by cab. If he had any doubts about his work, they weren't discernible in his wisecracking, self-critical joking.

So it went for a year and a half. I had my evenings and weekends free, as well as odd days—more time off than most secretaries had. I could play some tennis, have guests for dinner, and get into trouble. I had a knack for finding men who turned out to be unmarriageable and broke my heart.

This time it was Norman. We met at night in a short-story class in a public high school. That a handsome textile broker (whatever that is) was taking a short-story class seemed prophetic. We walked away together.

A month later, one night in my apartment, his dark secret bloomed. Somewhere in Philadelphia a young wife and baby daughter were living with his parents, awaiting his every-other-weekend visits. For all his suave business dress and Gregory Peck good looks as he sidled into my house every night, except the thirteenth and fourteenth ones, he increasingly bore the mark of a man to whom guilt was fed steadily every other weekend, along with his Rice Krispies. Here were all the ingredients of a killer romance.

"But how do you know a man is married if he doesn't tell you?"

"You know, you know," said Alan. "They're more attractive."

Howard's reaction came in the mail:

Dear Dottsie,

Wish you were here. As a matter of fact wish I were there. We'd have fun.

Maybe I'll make it all right in February. Romantic love is a kind of poison, a genuwyne narcotic.

I don't know what the hell to write except I want to send in this letter greetings, felicitations, love from the outerworld, the outerworld which is implacable, not as warm, and not nearly as intense as the little dark cocoon of love. . . . The world where, barring accidents, nothing of tremendous importance is going to happen from day to day. The only thing of genuine importance that can happen is the slow unfolding of a major pattern. It's painful as hell to jump from the thrill-a-minute action-packed, extreme, and simplified hot little world of love (see if you can set that to music).

I wish you and I were walking up Fifth Ave. to the Museum. Paintings are those little intense private (only sharable) worlds too. I hope you will try writing a lot. There has to be some way of bringing life to intense focal points. Art does that as well as love. Of course both would be great.

For a man who feels guilty, as Norman does, and oppressed by problems he's not handling, falling in love is a wonderful escape. All of a sudden there is something of such overshadowing importance that nothing else matters, and he is momentarily excused from conscience and debt. If this is simply a device, it has to be done again and again, but if there is some real basis for it, the man eventually ends up with all the old problems grown worse and conflicting new ones to boot. This can quite possibly produce coma, which gets him off the hook for a while, while the partner, still vitally conscious, is quite vulnerable.

Vell den, keep a stiff upper lip, and smile, as the doctor said to Alec Guinness after telling him he was going to die. *(The Last Holiday)*

More soon, your loving brother, H.

As I folded the precious thing in the envelope, I got a whiff of the fresh, amusing outer world from inside the little dark cocoon of love, where I, too, was slipping into a coma. Norman wasn't Howard's kind of a man.

To help me get over my bondage to Norman, I went to see Dr. Joe Barnett. After six months I got the courage to give Norman his guitar and clean shirt to take home. One day I said to Dr. Barnett: "I've met two men."

"Which one do you like best?"

"I think I like the tall dark writer who asked me to lunch."

"Who's the other one?"

"He's a kind of rugged, sensitive-looking documentary filmmaker."

"I'll make you a bet," Dr. Barnett said from his chair.

"I know," I said, "the writer for lunch is married."

He was.

The other, Bert, hadn't called me since I met him three weeks before, when he appeared one sunny day on the tennis courts at Rockefeller University on the river. We were a party of five: my old friends from California, Joe and Sunny, married; Harry Robbins, divorced already, and his filmmaking colleague, this fellow Bert.

He came on the courts in white shorts, with slim hips, dark gold hair which had begun to recede above a long, complicated, tense, handsome face. He was very male.

We played doubles, alternating among the five of us. Bert reached up high and slammed his serves. He wiped his face with a crumpled handkerchief.

After tennis we all went to have lunch in a coffee shop. Watching Bert herd us into the booth, I could envision him calling to the juniors at camp for tennis or swimming periods. I watched his upper lip mash down upon his flared, sculpted lower lip into a smile, with crinkles at the corners.

But he wasn't smiling at me. He was smiling at and animating Sunny, and I was chatting with Joe and Harry. Joe had a photographic memory; we were talking about his favorite ballerinas and performances he remembered.

The only thing Bert said to me as I got out of his green wood-slatted Chevy station wagon was "Take care," as in these days people say, "Have a good day."

But I had other things besides Bert to worry about. When I came up the carpeted stairs to my door, I found a note from Mr. and Mrs. Green, my landlords: The Fire Department had come and found my two-burner electric stove behind the screen. I didn't know it was a secret. But the firemen said I had to move; no more cooking there. It seemed like a message. I vowed that Norman would never cross my new threshold.

In those days finding an apartment was easier than finding tenants. I took a flat in the East Fifties with a large old cement terrace over a restaurant and a whole kitchen. Alan readily gave me time off to make the move. He was a peach.

One night, as I was sitting among the cartons, the phone rang. I recognized Bert's slightly formal tenor voice.

"I've been out of town shooting a film," he said. "Can I see you? What are you doing now?"

"Packing," I said. "I'm moving."

"Maybe I can help you," he said.

I accepted the mystery of his reappearance. Within minutes he was there, going about the room, peering at Howard's paintings and drawings still on the walls. He studied each one, while I sat studying him. I had always been a sucker for beauty. He looked a little like Prince Philip.

At length he said, "We'll have to take these carefully in the car." He was taking charge.

He handled them easily, but like the precious things they were. We stacked them one by one in the back seat of his station wagon and drove over to the new apartment. In the next days he brought a toolbox and put nails in places we both chose and hung my pictures on the white walls. It was beginning to look like home. My California furniture looked light, low, and slim, and pleased me. I would be settled in time for my mother's forthcoming visit.

Alan had said, "Order a limousine and go out and meet her."

My mother came off the plane with her hat and eye veil tilted, just as her head was, toward the adventure she was having coming to New York all on her own. Her eyes rolled with modest delight as the chauffeur held the door open to the big black car.

That night, at a table in a restaurant, she tumbled into love with Bert. Not only was he the first eligible man she had seen me with, but he was being eminently hostly, generous, and solicitous, like a son on Mother's Day. He had chosen a candle-lit restaurant. Her romantic nature basked. My romance was hers.

When we left her at her hotel that night, she reached up and kissed Bert on the cheek.

I still hadn't kissed him, nor he me.

In the next week Bert carried bags of sheep dung up to my second-floor terrace. He mixed, he planted, we rode around in his station wagon; we went to pay a visit to his dusty office on Forty-fifth Street, which he shared with another filmmaker, and he took me to dinners. Days and days went by, the flowers started to bloom, and he still wouldn't kiss me.

One night it got late. We were sitting on the couch. Bert suddenly stood up, doing stomach exercises for tension.

"Let's get in the car and drive out to the beach," he said. I thought: I don't want to go to the beach. I said so. We looked at each other. There was nothing else to do. He kissed me; his arms went around me. His mouth was so sweet, so deep and strong. I knew I was going to love him. And have him.

Unwinding from me, he drew back, and standing off by the terrace door, he uttered four words that I would always re-member.

"Careful" was what he said, with his head down. "I'm very emotional."

I don't know how I knew, but in that moment, as he looked at me, it was clear as a magic crystal that he was offering me his love and loyalty for the rest of his mortality. I experienced a glowing moment of illumination, in which I perceived the immense privilege of marriage. He was going to give me the chance to live an emotional life. An intimate life. Touch. Be my best friend. Farewell to empty beds. My romantic quest was coming to rest.

As I took his slender, powerful hand in mine, I got ready to say good-bye to all others.

So what happened? Nothing happened. I couldn't bring myself to undress in front of Bert just then. I needed time. I said my first lie to him: "My mother is still in town. I wouldn't want to have to lie to her tomorrow morning. Can we wait?"

He reached out, and I felt his warm hand on my face. "That's just like you," he said. "I love you for it."

Two days later, in the middle of the Fourth of July weekend, we took my mother to the airport and headed upstate to Finger Lakes country and to a bed, with no hotel reservations.

As we drove the miles up the highway, we would interrupt the rapt silence between us from time to time.

I found out Bert was no pussycat. He had dropped bombs on Japanese bridges and headquarters and navigated aircraft in the north of China with the Flying Tigers during the war. When he came home, he entered law school, thinking he would defend the underdog, but he soon became disillusioned with the big-business aspects of law. So he switched to film school. He had shot a film about Helen Keller. The three-week trip he took when I first met him was to write and direct a film about the Special Forces with General Powell in Virginia for the Army Pictorial Center. He had traveled all over, making documentary films for network series on science. I gathered the world was his oyster; he could do films on any subject he wanted, as long as he could write the proposal and get the grant.

I loved driving in the country with him. The sun was disappearing to our left. I felt the gladness of a summer evening approaching. We had some low green mountains ahead. I listened to Bert.

If he'd had his way, we all would be socialists, out of humaneness, but his active political days were over. Although he went on a march once, he never joined a movement.

He thought all organized religion was a fraud.

"I had to interview Cardinal Spellman," he said with a wry smile. "It was an event at St. Patrick's Cathedral. I was standing waiting my turn. When I reached him, he put out his pudgy hand for me to kiss his ring. I shook hands with him instead."

I laughed and reached out to him behind the wheel and stroked the back of his neck and played with the short, curly hairs that seemed to continue on down to his back. He nuzzled my hand. I reminded myself that I would soon see that back for the first time.

"Pretty soon we'll be at the lakes, and we'll stop and call for a place to stay and have dinner. Are you hungry?"

I don't remember where we ate that night, but at one point, after the sun had set and night had fallen, the highway turned to country road. In each town we came to, Bert would get out of the car and go to a lit phone booth on the main street as I watched from the car. He made three or four brief calls in each. "No vacancy" was always the answer. The motels we passed in the darkness continued to proclaim in flashing lights that they had no room. It got late. We went on. The country was resort and rural. In the sky we saw fireworks.

It was after midnight. It felt like northern country. I wanted that bed anywhere. But Bert wanted that bed on the lake. Now he was on the phone, and somebody at the other end finally had something to talk about. The only sound on the silent street was Bert's clear voice from inside the phone booth. He was saying, "Yes, yes," and looked at me in the car. Then I heard him say, "Is it on the lake?"

We drove about a mile to a sleeping group of low buildings, following some instructions Bert had taken down on a small piece of folded paper filled with cryptic notes.

Under a full moon we tiptoed in the glow behind someone who led us to a door of what seemed to be a cabin. There was a big bed, and by going to the far corner of the room, looking out the window, we could indeed see a little portion of lake in the moonlight.

That night, behind the locked door, in our privacy, I learned of Bert's givingness and mine. As two days ago his mouth was so sweet, so strong, so deep, so was the whole Bert. By night's end his slight formality had turned to a quiet, unstated possession of me. I was in the warm, intense little dark cocoon of love, and Bert was in it with me.

In the morning we went to search for a quiet breakfast. Following signs, we opened a door and found we had landed in the heart, rather the stomach, of a full-blown, clamorous resort hotel dining room. Hundreds of people were sitting and chattering at round tables. A large buffet, bearing a cornucopia of smoked salmon and bagels and cream cheese, platters of scrambled eggs, and Russian coffee cake, was spread out near the little stage. We joined a table of ten. A master of ceremonies was announcing somebody's birthday, anniversary, telling us where to get canoes, announcing children's activities, sauna hours, tennis court sign-ups. We sat holding hands, amused, shedding light from our secret of the night before, which nobody noticed.

In the afternoon Bert found us a canoe, and we paddled out across the lake to a far little island. A short distance off, through trees, people were having a picnic. We settled in the woods, made more love. Bert built a small fire and made the little wilderness on the lake ours before going home to the city.

The next morning, back in town, we parted on the street. Bert kissed me and said, for the first time, a phrase whose meaning would change: "Have fun."

I would rather he had said: Come with me.

He added, "Will I see you tonight?"

II

Something was going on in the country at Alan's that in my preoccupied and inexperienced state I was only vaguely aware of. Alan didn't call for several days.

One late summer morning that 1954, while I was sitting around the office talking to Bud, the door flew open, and Lerner and Loewe burst in, bristling with creative jubilance, Fritz's eyes melancholy and mischievous and Alan's, shrewd, clever, and youthful under his emotional eyebrows.

"We've solved *Pygmalion*!"

I didn't know they were trying.

Bud gave a great cry of "Yea!" and I said congratulations, but I remember having the brilliant thought that turning *Pygmalion* into a musical would ruin it. It was one of my favorite plays, and I thought the movie with Leslie Howard and Wendy Hiller literate, complete, perfect. That night at dinner Bert agreed with me. And Howard, on the phone from Santa Barbara, said to Bert, "How dare they touch Shaw?"

So much for ignorance. Nevertheless, they went ahead without our approval.

"My boy," said Fritz, putting his hand on Alan's shoulder, "shall we make the call?"

"We" meant Alan, the spokesman, the negotiator. Alan handed me a slip of paper.

"Put in a call to Rex Harrison in London, will you, dear?"

Henry Higgins! I thought.

They disappeared into Alan's office and closed the door.
From that day on whatever doubts or fears they might have
had were invisible in the gaiety and camaraderie between them.
They embarked on the long journey as one bold spirit. For the
entire adventure I never saw a moment of pique or impatience
or even stress. They were two gallants when they were together.

When Herman Levin came back from Europe, he found he
had inherited the show of the century. With his help Alan
immediately got out of *Li'l Abner,* in return for which he gave
Herman Levin the right to produce the show that became *My
Fair Lady.*

When it was time for Lerner and Loewe to move into the
city, Fritz took rooms at the Algonquin Hotel, and the Lerners
rented a furnished town house in the East Eighties. From my
seat across from Alan, in the country house, later in the city
house, at the Algonquin, and then next to him in the dark
theater during auditions and rehearsals, I witnessed and re-
corded *My Fair Lady* accumulating around me. On several late
nights Alan would say to me about my separation from Bert,
"More fuel for the fire."

Whatever Alan and Fritz did together was a total mystery
to me. They worked like one expanded person. They would
go into a room, stay for hours, and come out with the goods.
Alan's soft, crisp, careful voice would deliver the words to me,
piece by delicious, luscious piece, and to my delight, they kept
coming out sounding like George Bernard Shaw. I would take
them down in shorthand, read them back, then type them.

When a new song was finished, Lerner and Loewe would
play and sing it to me. I was probably the first person to hear
these beauties.

Bert had more or less moved into my apartment—shirts and
jackets and slacks and all—but on nights when I worked late,

he would go back to his, in Greenwich Village. He accepted my few late nights from the very beginning. He was so even-tempered I could do anything I liked. We had a group of friends, and on weekends one of us gave dinner parties, at which, as rumors spread that the new Lerner and Loewe show was going to be a smash hit, the conversations always began with "How's the show?" Bert and I went to concerts and theater and on long weekends went away in the car.

Unaware of danger, Bert and I were developing a style that was better suited to courtship than to the marriage we were heading for. While three of our friends had babies, we were adapting to the demands of the show and also to Bert's free-lance trips which lasted from two or three days or even two weeks. I dreaded the good-bye kiss and the sound of him going down the stairs with his camera, and I felt lonely coming home. But the excitement of Alan and the writing of the show was never more than a night's sleep away. It was my first Broadway musical. My snobbery had been left far behind. The script was getting thicker in my lap. I felt the thrill of *My Fair Lady* becoming. And of the return kisses at the end of Bert's trips. I was having the best of it all.

So fascinating were these days that the whole chancy nature of the production merely grazed my consciousness. That Lerner and Loewe were writing for months without the rights from the Shaw estate, or that Rex Harrison was offering stiff resistance to their long-distance courting, never for a moment intruded on my fairyland experience of this show. Then they went off to London for six weeks and came back triumphant, with rights, Rex, Cecil Beaton for costumes, Stanley Holloway for Alfred Doolittle, and Robert Coote for Pickering. The young English actress Bert and I had loved in the off-Broad-way *The Boyfriend* was hired to play Eliza. She was Julie Andrews. Moss Hart materialized to direct.

At auditions, from the seat of a dark theater, I watched the show gather dancers and singers into the cast, Alan charming and courtly with his colleagues.

One winter day, shortly before rehearsals began, Rex Harrison arrived from England and came to Alan's house. Fritz played, and Rex sang. It was awful. He croaked; he sort of yowled. He was angry and frightened and wondered in an agonized voice how the devil he'd ever gotten into the mess of agreeing to do a musical.

I was alarmed. I suddenly realized the fragility of this project; its whole future seemed threatened.

But Lerner and Loewe knew better. They would go with Rex into Alan's studio downstairs, and from the next room, within a few days, I began to hear Rex master the speak-sing patter and declamation that Henry Higgins would make famous.

And then, finally, we were in rehearsal, where Moss Hart reigned. Elegant, gentlemanly, funny, biting, anecdotal, he would stride into the theater in his mink-lined vicuña coat, and there would be friendly, creative huddles between him and Lerner and Loewe.

I sat next to Alan in the dark and took notes and went out to Lindy's on the corner for lots of coffee and sandwiches. I watched *My Fair Lady* come to life in fragments onstage.

In my star-struck state I thought everybody was equal. I didn't realize that Julie Andrews wasn't a star yet and that she was frightened to play to Rex Harrison, who was on edge himself, and that she was shy about exploding her brash Eliza Doolittle against his Higgins.

After rehearsal Moss Hart would work with her privately, and Alan and Fritz would coach her in the songs. As rehearsals progressed and Eliza Doolittle turned from a guttersnipe into a duchess, I saw Julie grow into a star.

By the time *My Fair Lady* was ready to try out in New Haven, Bert and I had been engaged and living together for a year and a half, and the whole company knew it. Bert was leaving it up to me to say when we would marry.

As the train pulled out, I waved good-bye to him through the window. His coat collar was up, his hatbrim down; there was a smile on his face and pain in his eyes. My heart sank. Fritz Loewe was standing next to me. He said, "When are you two going to get married?"

"As soon as we get back," I said.

The day of the opening night in New Haven there was a blizzard. All sorts of theater people were coming up from New York. The word was that something special was going to happen that night. But the blizzard covered the town.

A few days before, the orchestra replaced the rehearsal piano. Rex faced the conductor and musicians below and in front of him and was thrown for a loop by the noise of the instruments. A rumor spread that he had refused to go on. There was talk of postponing the opening. I was too inexperienced to have a point of view; I just listened. Behind closed doors, pressures, which I heard about only afterward, were brought to bear.

At eight o'clock, despite the blizzard, the theater was full, the curtain went up, and Rex was onstage, yammering and clattering to Julie and about to sing "Why Can't the English?" for the first time before an audience. At what cost we'll never know, he became a musical Henry Higgins: arrogant, crotchety, disdainful, and a great star from that moment until the final "Where the devil are my slippers, Eliza?," when the curtain came down.

I was in tears. You can imagine the excitement in the theater.

Except, according to Alan and Moss Hart, something was wrong.

A meeting was called in Alan's suite. All the magicians came: Moss Hart; Cecil Beaton; Oliver Smith, the designer;

Goddard Lieberson, an old friend who was going to produce
the record for Columbia; Hanya Holm, the choreographer. All
but Fritz were worried. He kept smiling and saying, "We have
a hit, we have a hit."

There was a hubbub of suggestions, and the whole play lay
open for dissection. Alan didn't say a word; he listened.

Early the next morning he called me in my hotel room.
"Would you like to come down?" he said cheerily. "Bring
your script."

He looked rested amid the bedlam from the night before. He
hadn't put the room service carts out in the hall. His voice was
sure and steady as with the deceptive simplicity of genius, he
softly dictated a completely new scene. This was turning out
to be Alan at his peak.

I went to the typewriter. The scene was so short it took only
a few minutes. I typed it in awe. He snatched it from my hands
and read it, and with a slight rearrangement of words, the new
scene for *My Fair Lady* came to life. That clinched it for me.
My devotion to Alan was set in cement.

What he had realized was that we didn't see Eliza Doolittle
go to the ball. After her disaster at Ascot a montage of scenes
in Higgins's study was directly followed by the ballroom, with
ladies in gorgeous Cecil Beaton creations strolling about.
When Julie finally appeared looking only a little more beautiful than the others, the drama was missing.

Lerner's new scene also takes place in Henry Higgins's
study, but on the night of the ball. Higgins and Pickering are
pacing around, waiting for Eliza to finish dressing and appear.
Higgins refuses a glass of port wine for his nerves. When Eliza
finally enters at the top of the stairs, caught in Abe Feder's
lighting, with Fritz Loewe's music, in Cecil Beaton's masterpiece of a dress, she is transformed into a duchess. Higgins
watches her descend the stairs, gives her his arm, swoops up
his cloak, and, as they go to the door, turns back and takes a

gulp of port for his nerves. The second night, with the montage out and the new scene in place, the play was perfection.

Somewhere along the way Richard Maney, the show's publicist, promoted me from secretary to assistant to Alan Jay Lerner by listing me that way in the program. If Alan ever noticed the change, he never spoke of it. My family enjoyed the promotion, though.

We have moved the show to Philadelphia. I'm on the phone with Bert. He has awakened me in the hotel room. They've been polishing *My Fair Lady* into a jewel in preparation for the New York opening. I can hear Rex Harrison in the next room, pleading with and bullying room service, in his high-pitched British voice, for his breakfast. He is still on edge.

"When I hear your sleepy voice, I can imagine you in bed and I just want to dump this film and take the next plane to where you are," says my darling. "But I have to get one more shot this morning, and then I'll drive in. I'll be there tonight. Leave the key for me."

Bert didn't always get an inspirational film to do. This one, near Chicago, was a commercial picture for a garage door company.

"Drive so far?" I say. "Maybe you'd better stop over somewhere and come in tomorrow."

"I'll be there tonight," he says.

"I'm dying to see you."

It was the dead of winter. The first days of March. Bert felt he could cross any miles in his car.

I imagined him driving through snow and ice. I worried.

I never saw him that night. I only knew that at some time in the middle of the night I was lying underneath his warm and heavy body in the dark in our single bed. "I drove six hundred miles," he mumbled, and fell immediately into a deep sleep, and we didn't move until the morning.

I found out that day that Bert was a little spacey after he finished a film. As we waited for the elevator to go down to breakfast the next morning, Rex appeared from his room, tall, spindly, craggy. He and Bert shook hands.

"I hear you're doing the great deed," Rex said, looking partly appraisingly and partly commiseratingly at Bert. He had been married several times.

When I looked at Bert's perplexed face, I knew he had heard "the great deed" as the title of his next film. Some great deed or other would just suit Bert. Finally he answered, with a modest hand gesture, "No. I've just finished *The Overhead Door*."

On the day *My Fair Lady* opened in New York, Alan and I were sitting in his studio alone. Everybody had been invited and gotten his ticket. Gifts from Cartier, with notes for the stars, were wrapped and on their way to their dressing rooms. I had sent a limousine to meet Lillie at the airport and arranged for her suite at the Gotham Hotel. There was nothing more to do. "Thanks to you," said Alan.

That night, after the show opened to a euphoric audience, we went to Alan's mother's apartment. In his book, Alan talked about an opening night party at 21. He may well have gone there later, but first he went to his mother's house. Among the guests I was there with Bert. We were going to be married the next month, in April.

So here we were at Edie Lerner's, Bert in a tux, I in a gown, sitting under her crystal chandelier in the dining room over Park Avenue, waiting for the newspaper reviews. When they arrived, somebody handed them to me. As I read them out loud, there was a hush. Alan flushed. Though he was a terrific snob, he was humble about his work. Fritz, with his fine European head and expressive mouth, beamed, a little smugly.

After I finished reading, we sat with our mouths open.

Before anyone had a chance to say anything, Alan's mother took center stage, exactly like the "large Wagnerian mother with a voice that shatters glass" that Alan wrote about in Henry Higgins's song "Let a Woman in Your Life."

"What, my son," she boomed, "can you ever do to top this?"

Nobody spoke. Presently Alan gave a little laugh and looked down at his hands. But her words haunted him ever after. He never did top *My Fair Lady.* And why should he have to? He wasn't climbing a ladder. But a fear of humiliation followed him, and as time passed, he had a recurring nightmare in which he saw the audience seated in the theater, the orchestra starting to play, the curtain going up, and nothing but a bare, empty stage in front of them. I know, because he later told me so.

A few days before our wedding Bert closed out his apartment in Greenwich Village and came up the stairs, bearing a big old green easy chair, a souvenir of his bachelorhood, which he deposited in the middle of my slim living room. I said, "Please take it out."

"We can have it re-covered if you like," said Bert, sitting in the chair as though it were his island.

After all was said and done, I thought, I was going to vow on Sunday to live with only Bert for the rest of my life, never again to be charmed by the angle of a male chin, a swagger, a growth of black stubble on a new face.

I was wearing the gold lamé caftan he had brought me one night in a Bonwit Teller box loaded with tissue paper. I had put it on to please him, though I would have preferred a silk kimono or a terry-cloth wrap to this movie star clothing. I wondered how he imagined our life, with my gold caftan and his green chair. It never occurred to me that maybe Bert needed the green chair to join my furniture.

"Please take it away," I said. "I hate it." He did.

We had hired a rabbi for Sunday, planned a big party after-

ward, and invited all our friends and relatives to come. The
Lerners were coming. My parents were arriving from California.

If Bert had any jitters himself, he didn't tell me. At the
wedding he stood with his hand on my bare arm and, when
it was time, slid the ring onto my finger with a sexy little
gesture and a smile, giving me a sudden thrill. This was real.
I was in the act of becoming a wife. Bert's wife. We would have
and hold each other from now on.

But he left me. The next morning at six-thirty he got out
of bed, showered and dressed, and went to Boston. I was alone
on a rainy Monday, April 23. I sat in the bed in the gray room
and watched the puddles forming on the terrace floor. Flowers
from the day before and the ring on my finger were the only
evidence that anything had happened. Bert had his film to do
at MIT and his crew to have dinner with, but I had given up
my job and between one day and the next had no more *My Fair
Lady* or Alan or Fritz or Bud to go to in the office.

I had said good-bye to Alan at the party yesterday.

"You'll be back," he said knowingly. "When are you leaving?"

"Not for a month—end of May," I said, laughing at my
predicament. "And Bert is going to Boston tomorrow."

"You're going with him, of course."

"They start shooting at seven in the morning. They don't
come back till six. Can you see me sight-seeing alone in Boston
the day after our wedding? Besides, my parents are here. I'm
taking them to the show tonight."

"Doris, Doris," the king of romantic plotting said, shaking
his head, "that would never play."

As I struggled against the depressing letdown, I reminded
myself that it was only temporary. We had a whole summer
to look forward to, Bert and I, in California.

I was gloomily looking out of the window when the phone rang. It was Alan.

"What are you doing? Do you want to go on an interview with me?"

"Yes, I do."

So it went. Though I had married Bert, my fate would be tied to Alan for ten more years.

My friend Joe had said to me, "Life with Bert will be an adventure."

Our extravagant honeymoon began on the strikingly brilliant sunny and unseasonably cool morning of May 30, when Bert and I loaded up the station wagon and closed the door on our emptied apartment.

The whole country lay before us on his lap in the green and blue colors of the map. We were going across it. Bert was navigator.

As we left New Jersey behind and entered rolling Pennsylvania, all the future I could imagine was just this one long holiday. I didn't know what we had done to deserve it.

Sitting still while the car carried us at sixty and sometimes seventy miles an hour through the middle rural states in early June, shunning the big cities, we were lulled by the soothing monotony and fragile privacy of our car. Every day, around three o'clock in the afternoon, Bert would pull up to a motel on the outskirts of a town, each one more western than the day before. We swam in almost the same swimming pool and walked to the same recommended restaurant, only grazing the town itself with our presence.

I got a thrill each day when Bert signed "Mr. and Mrs. Bert Shapiro" at the desk. I had not yet had to come to grips with the change from Doris Warshaw to Doris Shapiro.

In the mornings, with the sun rising behind us, we talked

as we drove through the spaces of New Mexico, with its red earth and blue sky. It became clearer to me that Bert and I felt the same way about the world; only he knew more. We had the same friends and enemies in public life; only he could articulate why.

"I can't imagine living with a man who doesn't go for Adlai Stevenson," I said. "Or even working for one. Did you know Alan is a Democrat?"

"He'll never win, though," Bert said. "He's too civilized, too literate. Here, I'll drive for a while; pull up."

We changed places at the side of the highway, with cars speeding past us.

"I worked for the Hollywood for Stevenson Committee four years ago," I said, settling into the comfort of the passenger seat. "I didn't realize what was going on in Hollywood at that time until Darryl Zanuck, the head of Twentieth Century-Fox, actually made it dangerous for his directors and actors to be on Stevenson's side. He put out a notice that he didn't want anyone at the studio to make appearances for Stevenson. Richard Widmark defied him. He did a film for our committee. But Frank Rosenberg, who was a director at Twentieth, after thinking it over for two days, turned down my invitation to a party to meet Stevenson. And do you know what he said to me?"

"No."

"He said, 'You know I love Stevenson, but I wouldn't want to hurt Darryl.' *Hurt* Darryl! I never went out with him again."

One evening we were having dinner on the patio of our Spanish hotel in Santa Fe. There were tiled terra-cotta floors, and the last of the sun was playing on the tops of the filigreed black wrought iron against the high white stucco walls, where hibiscus bloomed. Three Mexicans were playing mariachi music. June air softened the twilight, and Bert's face in the candlelight glowed as if he were a bottomless source of sweet life. I suddenly choked up and reached for him across the table.

Death brushed me, the ultimate abandonment.

"Promise me you won't die."

"Dotty!"

The house in Malibu, which my parents had found for us, was on the beach. It was a summer of family reunion, increase, and celebration, what with Howard's new wife, Franny, and my new husband, Bert, with trips up to Santa Barbara to stay with them (Howard was now a professor at the university there, painting a mural and playing polo) and to San Francisco to see Bert's flying buddy from the China days.

California life blotted out New York. I had taken to wearing a sarong and bare feet in and out of the house and beach. Bert had taken to calling me "sweetie."

Lillie and Alex had found a buyer for their Wright house and moved to a luxurious bungalow in the fancy heart of Beverly Hills. There was no room for Marlene Dietrich to stay anymore, and they were being careful with the grocery shopping. Nevertheless, they insisted on an evening out as their guests at the Luau. As we sat sipping rum drinks among the fake palms and tribal drums in the Hawaiian restaurant, I was eager to hear any news of Alan. Lillie mentioned that he had bought off her percentage of all his future profits by giving her a one-time payment. He had taken on the powerful Irving Lazar to be his agent. Her face in the glow of the hurricane lamp looked hurt.

To make it up to Lillie, Alan put her on salary. He never admitted it, but I knew he needed her. She did a lot of sticky things for him, using her contacts to do the impossible with hotel reservations, then last-minute cancellations, passing on astrological advice from the guru of Hollywood, being his personal representative with both public and private people, worshiping his talent without losing her critical eye.

"What are your plans when you go back to New York, Dotty?" Lillie said, looking at both Bert and me.

Even in warm California you can see by the light over the ocean when the summer is drawing to a close. We were leaving in a week. Lillie's question made me uneasy. I didn't have any plans. I had merely assumed that having left Alan for three months, I had forfeited my job. Surely by now he would have hired someone else.

"I haven't really thought about it," I said, without energy. "Be Bert's wife, I guess. We have to get an apartment."

Lillie leaned forward. I could tell she was on assignment. "Alan called me," she said. "He's going to call you."

"He is?" I felt a thrill but kept it to myself.

Early the next morning there was Alan's voice on the phone: sassy, chummy, affectionate, coaxing.

"When are you coming back?"

"We're leaving next week."

"How soon can you be here?"

"We're driving. Bert has to stop to interview an astronomer at Mount Wilson." I had already begun to wonder what I'd do at the motel at the bottom of the mountain while Bert went to the telescope at the top three days in a row.

"How would you like to work for your love Adlai Stevenson? With me."

Would I! I flipped.

"I've agreed to get all the entertainment people for the whole campaign," said Alan.

Two days later I was on the plane, with Bert's blessing. He had said, "You can fly back if you want, and I'll drive."

"Drive all alone, all the way?" I said.

"I can do it in four days."

From the beginning I accepted Bert's indulgent attitude

about my job. There was no harm done to anybody until much
later.

One condition: I was to put all my checks in the savings
bank, and we'd live on what Bert made. It seemed innocent
enough.

Alan said to me, "Don't ever go away like that again."

By the time Bert arrived in the station wagon, I already had
a nice little apartment on Seventy-second Street off Park Avenue, one month's rent free, furniture out of storage and in
place, except for Howard's paintings, awaiting Bert's hammer.
It was so easy to make a home.

This was 1956, before the great television takeover of poli-
tics. Alan put his heart into the phone, charming loads of stars
to go to rallies around the country. Adlai Stevenson never did
become president. But someone must have noticed Alan, because five or six years later he would be asked to produce a
birthday party for President Kennedy.

In between *My Fair Lady* and *Gigi,* Alan's marriage to
Nancy had not gone well. She was his third wife. When he first
met her, I had heard, Alan used to haunt her dressing room at
the studio with gifts and flowers. He courted this lovely Nor-
dic blonde from the Middle West with ardor. If she ever wondered what she did to set all his passion loose, she never seemed
to show it or even know it. She would come home in the
evening, go into the bathroom and take off her makeup and
clothes and put on a little housecoat. Showing her natural face,
no longer delineated and highlighted by makeup, she'd sigh
with pleasure and say, "How I love to take my makeup off."
But she had a poignancy on the screen that revealed depths he
must have suspected.

One day Alan mentioned to me, as if it were a personal
injury, that Nancy's face was puffy when she woke up in the

morning. Another day he turned away in quiet anger when she
asked him to talk to the director of the play she was rehearsing
with whom she was having trouble.

They continued to move to larger and grander apartments.
Nancy's mother had told her that the three crises in a woman's
life were getting married (she had succeeded brilliantly), having a child (she had two), and furnishing her first home. This
was now a vast one-story apartment on Fifth Avenue in the
Eighties, with eight or so living-room windows facing the
park. It was her project to furnish it. Nancy went out with her
mentor-decorator every day. Now she and Alan had much to
talk about: the furnishing of the apartment. She was having her
third crisis, but it wasn't Alan's. He was about to start *Gigi*.

The collaboration of Lerner and Loewe was still thriving
when they began *Gigi* for the movies. Fritz hadn't had his
heart attack.

MGM was going to go all out. Maurice Chevalier, the great;
Louis Jourdan, the suave and handsome; Leslie Caron, the
adorable star of Alan's *An American in Paris;* and Hermione
Gingold, for the grandmother were all signed.

Colette's story of an adolescent girl being groomed to
become a brilliant courtesan to the blasé, cynical men of Paris
was perfect for Alan's witty, ironical, and even nasty lyrics,
and, when Gigi blooms and Gaston finally falls for her and
offers his hand in marriage, perfect for Alan's tender and in-
love lyrics. Lerner and Loewe started working on songs that
would turn Colette's Paris into Lerner and Loewe's Paris.

To celebrate the start of the script, we drove out one spring
day to the country house. There was dogwood blooming.
Snug in the little studio in the woods, with everything fresh—
clipboards, yellow paper, manicuring implements, and toilet
water—Alan spoke the first words in a soft, decisive voice.

"Scene One," he said. "The Bois de Boulogne. A clear
summer day."

Now he was in for it, I thought. He had taken the perfect unity of the blank page and tossed it into chaos. He had to resolve it.

I thought, with a thrill: Go get the Parisian woods on a clear summer day.

"Turn of the century," he said carefully.

And on that clear summer day, go get the polished, decorated carriages and horses in place and ready to roll for the camera.

"All Parisian high society is out for a ride or a stroll."

Alan had an amused, pleased, somewhat devil-may-care look around his mouth as he waited for me to react.

Go, I thought, get Cecil Beaton to put into his workshops the scores and scores of outfits to adorn the beauties who would wear them.

By the time I had filled one third of my first yellow page with notes, as we sat three thousand miles from either Paris or Hollywood, he had spent a fortune and set all the wizards loose in the woods. Alan loved to spend money, to make all these things happen. He was happy.

The writing of *Gigi* went smooth as silk.

One day Nancy went with the children and nurse to California to visit her parents. While she was gone, workmen came with drapes for the windows. Many drapes. They spent hours hanging them. When they were all up, Alan and I went to see them. They were aqua, yards and yards of aqua hanging from the windows.

"Impossible," he said. "Take them down. Take them away."

When Nancy called that night, he consoled her. "Don't worry, darling, we'll get others. I don't mind. Everybody gets to make one big mistake."

"But you took them down before I could even see them!"

As it turned out, the apartment never got any drapes. But I don't think Alan planned it that way then.

Most of *Gigi* was going to be shot in Paris, some of it in Maxim's, using the fountains, the boulevards, the parks, and, as we said, the Bois de Boulogne. Alan called from Paris as if he were next door. One day he invited me to come. Bert said, "Go, you've never been to Paris."

But rumors were coming back daily that Alan had fallen wildly in love with a Frenchwoman. According to the papers, she was on the set every day with him and the company constantly. I was dying to go, but I felt a little guilty about Nancy, whose New York world was falling apart, staying home. I needn't have. When she read that her marriage was disappearing, she complained that he didn't need me over there with him, too. Eager to give her some small solace, Alan called me from across the ocean and told me not to come. For my revenge, knowing that he hated to be reminded he was Jewish, I said on the transatlantic phone, "All right, but hereafter, all Jewish holidays off." I unpacked, and Bert and I went out to dinner.

When Alan came home, he had his new lady love with him. I had never seen Alan in love before. As I stood in the black silk jersey chemise I had chosen for the occasion, hand outstretched, with my friendliest smile, Alan, filled with amorous energy but a bit snobby, said, "The future Mrs. Lerner." I knew her name to be Micheline: Micheline Muselli Pozzo di Borgo. One glance at this small-boned French Corsican lady lawyer, who could have been the original Dior model, and I knew that Nancy was no match. Her handshake was stronger than I expected from the golden flow of hair and the upturned, almost childlike mouth. Although her teeth showed when she acknowledged me, it wasn't exactly a smile, and her eyes were dangerous.

"I wish you much happiness," I said to her.

"*Oui,*" she said. "We're so in love. Alain," she called lovingly to him across the room, where he had returned to Irving Cohen, his lawyer, who was sitting on the couch handling some papers. There was something legal going on.

"I hope this is all right," I said, indicating the lavish apartment I had taken for them at the Stanhope Hotel. Uptown, discreet, grandly residential, the rooms overlooked Fifth Avenue and the park from about the fifth floor, revealing the city panorama.

"Yes. Thank you," she said, not thanking me, but looking me up and down openly. We stood there.

"I hope you don't mind," I said, breaking away, "if I use the phone. I have to call my husband." Yes, yes, I thought, I was doing just the right thing.

"Darling?" I said to a surprised Bert, whom I had left a short time ago. "I'm coming home soon. I miss you."

When I hung up, Micheline said to me, this time smiling, "You must tell me where you got that charming dress."

Two days later they moved to the red, gold, and black St. Regis on teeming Fifty-fifth Street off Fifth. Soon after they moved again to a large, fully furnished apartment on Sutton Place. Alan changed houses easily. He simply had others come in and pack and move. He could leave an old home without nostalgia.

In spite of all this, *Gigi* got finished, and Lerner and Loewe took me with them to see it in a New York screening room.

Though I thought I knew every line of *Gigi*, I was totally unprepared for the dazzle of this work—its polish, charm, timing, extravagance, the perfect wedding of all the elements. The mastery of everyone involved. When the credits came up and the theater was filled with Frederick Loewe's music, my star-struck heart gave a thrust upward, and as the whole lavish scene in the sun and shadowy woods came to life in color, my eyes filled with tears. Though I was so familiar with the words on paper, when I saw the finished movie, with not a single misstep or lapse in mood or style, it was as if I'd never heard the story before.

I thought it was perfect, ready to go out into the world. But Lerner and Loewe said it wasn't. They wanted to reshoot the crowded scene in Maxim's and another small but critical scene on a little bridge in a park. MGM refused; it meant building a Maxim's set and a park set, which would cost three hundred thousand dollars. It meant getting Louis Jourdan and Leslie Caron back to Hollywood from far away places and other work. It meant filling Maxim's with revelers in costly costumes.

Lerner and Loewe went out to the studio and bluffed. They offered to put up the money themselves. They got their way. MGM relented, and after a few weeks construction on the lot began.

I didn't see the Maxim's scene, but Alan sent for me in Hollywood about the time they began making the scene in the little French park that was built on the lot, with water and swans and the bridge. As we stood watching the camera shoot Louis on the bridge, the swans kept unfurling their long necks and shaking their heads and splashing in the background. Alan kept whispering to me, "Those fucking swans."

III

By now Alan was married to Micheline, God save him. Nancy had moved with the children to the West Side Alan hated, and he was released from the ennui of his all-American marriage to a Middle American beauty from, he was apt to say, Scarsdale. I remember bringing Nancy some papers one day. She came out in a robe, still in a state of shock. What touched me was the way, with a certain wan little gesture, she passed her hand across her forehead, as if she were trying to clear her head of some painful image.

Alan had accumulated a staff, an office, an important accountant and a lawyer, who were busy on his behalf. He and Fritz were making fortunes since *My Fair Lady*. They had their Rolls-Royce convertibles (Alan's was royal blue with a beige top; Fritz's was gray), a fruit of the show. With them came chauffeurs. Alan's was Tony, an Italian lad who was writing a play for all the years I knew him.

One night, alone in his apartment at the Algonquin Hotel, Fritz had a mammoth heart attack. He knew he was going to have it; he had left the door open so someone could come and help.

Alan called me the next morning from the hospital. He thought Fritz might die. But three or four days later he and Micheline left Fritz in the hospital and went off to Europe.

Fritz came home from the hospital to a big suite at the Essex

House. I saw him pushed in a wheelchair with a blanket over his head by a ferocious nurse who kept urging him to speak French. He looked like a small immigrant getting off the boat. The ferocious nurse made his life miserable until he had the strength to get rid of her. Sick as he was, he could still be amusing about his predicament.

Before they left, Alan and Micheline had bought a house on Seventy-first Street between Madison and Park avenues next door to David Sarnoff. On the other side was the Tunisian Embassy, and down the block was Richard Rodgers's apartment in the big building at the corner of Park. A delicious block, a sweet red-brick house, with green shutters and a roof garden on the fifth floor. Nowadays it belongs to an institution.

Along with it came a household of servants. You had to speak a little French or they wouldn't understand you.

In that summer of the first year of the marriage, while Alan and Micheline were in Paris and on the island of Capri, the house on Seventy-first Street was transformed by armies on a deadline. The moldings on the walls were gold-leafed, the bathrooms marbleized, her bedroom voluptualized, with swans creating the sides of her bed; his, masculinized, was across the hall, so that he would have to travel whenever he felt moved to conquer. There was a good deal of gold satin furniture and leopard print carpet. Micheline wanted Napoleonic splendor for her New York house and modern New York in the Paris flat.

It was in this house that Micheline produced Alan's only son, Michael, who became the joy of his life. He already had three daughters. She regarded it as a triumph, declaring that producing a daughter didn't really count. Once, in a friendly moment, she told me I was the kind of female who would produce a son.

But it was Bert who produced a son. One night on my birthday he walked in carrying a little ball of fur, tucked into his raincoat. Dark baby eyes gazed softly out at me. I held out my arms.

We named him Teddy. This precious little presence was with us for the rest of my years with Alan. When he got his first haircut, he sprang into being as dark brown, with the curly hair, extravagant silken ears, long, slender snout, little trouser legs, and bunny tail that made him the handsomest poodle in the neighborhood. He grew to twenty-eight pounds, but that never stopped him from climbing onto Bert's lap.

For some reason he liked Alan, but Alan only tolerated him, giving him a swift pat on the head every now and then.

Recovered from his heart attack, Fritz was taking good care of himself, spending winters in his beloved Palm Springs and summers on the French Riviera. No more work.

But Alan wasn't happy. At the peak of his passion for Micheline, the luxurious pleasures of his new house and the adored presence of his baby son, Michael, he was driven to find a new show to do. He and Bud and Moss Hart were doing a lot of reading.

One day Bud, who now had his beard and pipe, ambled in with a review from *The New York Times* of *The Once and Future King,* by T. H. White.

Camelot!

This was no agonizing decision. It didn't require conferences with tycoons. Within two days of reading the four-volume book, which, if dropped on the foot, could break it, Alan Lerner and Moss Hart embraced the huge medieval tale of King Arthur and his Knights of the Round Table as light-heartedly as if setting all the powerful forces into motion that make a big Broadway musical were as easy as going off on a jaunt to jolly old England.

But Alan needed Fritz, had to have him. Fritz was no mere songwriter. He was the other half of Alan's theatrical sensibility.

Fritz, in New York at the moment, demurred. As winter approached, he was planning to take off for Palm Springs. But Alan was irresistible. Within a short time Fritz had succumbed. He would do the show, but he wasn't going to hurl his energies around the way he used to; he was going to guard his health. And Alan agreed to follow him to Palm Springs when winter came, to work there. Micheline had never been to Palm Springs.

Now, at the start of *Camelot,* Fritz seemed only one degree subdued: He brought his girl friend, Tammy, with him.

Tammy was a young actress. She didn't wear makeup. Her face was long, narrow, and white, with big dark eyes, and her straight black hair fell back from her forehead. Fritz's pet name for her was Tammy-boy. She was in love with him, but he refused to marry her because he said he was too old, and it was a foregone conclusion that one day she'd turn to someone else, and he wasn't about to walk into a betrayal. Fritz took better care of himself in love matters than Alan did.

After *My Fair Lady* and *Gigi,* Lerner and Loewe could do no wrong. They could have anybody and all the money they wanted. We took offices across the street from the Plaza Hotel. With Moss Hart directing, the three of them would produce.

First things first: Julie Andrews for Guinevere.

"Yes," she said ecstatically on the long-distance phone from London.

It was autumn, and I was working more hours than usual, but Bert and I didn't notice it. I had begun to realize he would always be coming and going, doing those civilized, open-handed films of the cosmos for public television that gave me the feeling there was order in the world and that somehow everything was all right: *The Realm of the Galaxies, Exploring the Milky Way, The Planets, No Place Like Earth,* and many others. Neither of us thought beyond the next trip. I was thankful Bert went away for only two or three weeks at a time.

His friend Bob was presently in the Amazon for two months. As for my going on the road with *Camelot,* it was almost two years off.

We lived a block from Alan's house on Seventy-first Street. In the early morning Bert would take Teddy for a run in the park. I would call Alan.

"Darling," he would say, picking up on the first ring. "How soon can you come?"

"Soon," I'd say.

"Hurry, hurry," he'd say. Alan hated to be alone.

Always when I went to Alan's I dressed as if for a date. He made me feel attractive, even beautiful. I loved him. Especially when he was in the throes of writing. I loved his shrewd, clever, good-natured, sensitive, deceitful eyes and twisted grin. I loved his dapper, energetic masculine frame, which I saw every day stripped to a bikini while he shaved. Alan was informal.

Most of all, I loved sitting in the big gilded chair in his bedroom, waiting for him to break out of a stuck scene or lyric, probing for the joke, the game, the classy turn of a phrase that would make history in the musical theater.

"There you are," Alan would say, smiling and looking up from his script, as I appeared at the door. "Sit down. Read the newspaper. I'll have something for you in a minute."

On those mornings, while Micheline was asleep across the hall, the early pages of *Camelot* emerged as a romantic romp through the Age of Chivalry. It didn't seem as if Fritz were holding back his energies, for the first scene alone had three humorous, romantic, effortless songs by which Arthur and Guinevere meet and are happily trothed.

Sometimes there would be a sound in the hall, and suddenly Michael, the little blond toddler, would appear and run up to his father, completing the escape from his latest nurse. Close behind, but stopping short at the doorway to Alan's bedroom,

she would reproach the baby and apologize to the father all at
once.

"That's all right," Alan would say to her, delighted by the
visit. "Come sit with me, Michael," he'd say, swinging the little
boy up onto his alcove bed. "He can stay with us for a while,"
Alan would say to the dispossessed nurse.

They would cuddle.

"What's your favorite word, Michael?" Alan said one day.

"Uh, I think"—the little baby face pondered with open
mouth—"island," he said.

Alan clasped him tenderly. "What a beautiful word, Michael."

Around midmorning Micheline would appear from Alan's
shower. Even in a towel, the scent of Shalimar preceded her.
She was very French, blond, sexy.

"He woke me up again." She pouted. "She lets him play and
run around the room over my head when I am sleeping." Her
English was laced with the crisp rat-a-tat-tat melodious phrasing of her native tongue.

"Get another nurse," Alan said.

"*Oui,*" she'd say, turning to go down the corridor that
connected their two rooms. "You go find one who isn't a
crook."

When she reentered, dressed as though about to take a turn
down Dior's runway, she'd ask Alan for pocket money; then
she'd go off with Tony, the chauffeur, to have her hair combed.
She was trying to establish herself with influential people, but
part of her toyed with the idea of acting school.

Once a week Alan would put down his clipboard and go
down to the music room, where he and Micheline would spend
an hour listening to Poulenc, Debussy, and Ravel, "to get away
from the Broadway music," as she said. Alan was in love.

Other interruptions in the writing came on the telephone
from Irving Cohen, the lawyer, about a shipment of couture

clothes arriving from Paris, which was turning out to be more than a tricky annoyance with the Customs Service.

Moss Hart on the phone one morning to Alan: "Richard Burton for King Arthur!"

Richard Burton calling back that afternoon from California: "Delighted."

Now Lerner and Loewe were writing for two stars.

All the right people were in place. Everybody was saying yes: Oliver Smith for the spooky woods sets, the Great Hall of the castle, the jousting field with tents, the queen's bedchamber, the battlefield. Hanya Holm for choreography.

Adrian, a famous costume designer, whom I remembered only for the big shoulders he dressed Joan Crawford in, would do the many royal costumes. Roddy McDowall presented himself to Alan, eager to play the evil Mordred. Robert Coote hooted with delight over playing King Pellinore, who wandered around the woods endlessly in search of his lost kingdom.

Only the gallant Lancelot remained to be cast. Nobody worried.

When winter came, Alan and his household followed Fritz to Palm Springs, as agreed. I stayed home. When they returned in spring, they were still writing cheery songs for the first act, like "The Lusty Month of May" and "Then You May Take Me to the Fair."

When summer came again, Fritz lured Alan and his family to the French Riviera. Bert and I, with Teddy, took a month or so in Santa Barbara, near Howard and his wife, Franny, and lived our other, California life, partly on horseback. We said one day we'd return.

It wasn't until the following summer in New York, 1960, with rehearsals near, that I became aware that darker tones were emerging in the play. Alan was writing adultery, betrayal by Arthur's beloved Guinevere and Lancelot, evil scheming by

Mordred, the deteriorization of the ideal of the Round Table, the specter of Guinevere being burned at the stake (an image that has always kept me away from Joan of Arc plays), war, and finally the vision of Arthur alone on the eve of battle, his Camelot redeemed by the appearance among the ruins of one small boy who believed.

As the dark threads appeared in the story, events in the writing and production of this show were already beginning to parallel them.

Adrian, the costume designer, died.

It was July. Rehearsals were to start September 3, but almost half of the play and songs were unwritten. The trick with this show had always been to choose the right amount of story from the four volumes to tell on a Broadway musical stage. The second act could be its downfall.

The Lerners took a house for the summer in Sands Point, Long Island, and Fritz took a small one nearby. The mansion, with a flaring staircase and high ceilings, overlooked the water, Alan hoped it would keep Micheline happy. It didn't. Although there was lots going on, with Fritz, Moss Hart, Bud Widney, Oliver Smith, and me, too, driving up in limousines and sleeping over, having meals in the vast dining room, and occasionally strolling around the big grounds and swimming in the pool, we always ended up disappearing into work sessions.

My Teddy loved to run after a ball on the lawn and play with Michael. But Micheline was restless, craved stimulation, adulation and dramatic events. Very tan from lying by the water, she was looking like a blond Carmen—and behaving like one. She was ready to defy and run off.

And that's what she did.

With nothing to do, one day she packed up her trunks and went off to Europe, taking with her the beloved son and his nurse. When she got to France, she called Alan to say they were never coming back.

The blow to Alan was so stunning that he needed psychiatric attention. He was mentally paralyzed and developed fierce migraine headaches. Work stopped. But we kept it a secret from Fritz, until a few days of medication and Alan's sheer professionalism brought him to finish the song Fritz was waiting to hear. I trace my obsession with Alan to this period.

I never for a moment doubted that he would bring the show in on time, though every word that accumulated seemed merely a drop in the ocean of the titanic script.

The three men—Lerner, Loewe, and Hart—went into rehearsal, behaving as if they were in a state of grace. A recovered Alan looked as chipper as if nothing had happened. Fritz was ever at his side. Moss Hart was nobly in charge, as we went into the theater on time.

Micheline, back from her abandonment, under what terms I didn't know, sat in the theater next to Alan and Fritz. I was in the seat in front of Alan. At home the servants were making preparations for Michael, his nurse, and Micheline's elderly French mother, an addition from Paris, to go on the road to Toronto and Boston.

From the first day Richard Burton dominated onstage and off. Everybody gravitated toward him and his voice, his playful improvisations, impersonations, and poetic recitations. Richard had yet to do his *Hamlet* in New York, and Elizabeth Taylor and *Cleopatra* were still in the future. He was a romancer, drank lots of whiskey, but never let anyone down.

Early on he befriended a young man from Tennessee named John Cullum, who sang in the chorus. John worshiped Richard, and Richard pushed for John to become his understudy. John Cullum would have a profound effect on a later Lerner show.

Bert came to dress rehearsal in New York. We were going to see the actors in their costumes for the first time. No expense was too much for the glories of *Camelot* that Adrian's replacement, Tony Duquette, had designed.

"Too dressy," Bert whispered to me.

"I agree," I said.

Bert ducked out toward the middle of the second act. That night at home he said to me, "The show is going to run four and a half hours. There's too much story to tell in the second act. Do you want to quit?"

"Oh, I couldn't." I put my arms around his neck. "But I love that you asked me."

Bert was prophetic. On opening night in the giant new O'Keefe Center in Toronto, the curtain went up at eight-fifteen, and it didn't come down until twenty of one in the morning.

Opening nights were Alan's torture. He might just as well walk naked down the aisle, surrounded by thirty-five hundred seated, expectant people.

Ten minutes before curtain time I went looking for him. My search led me backstage. In a far corner of the chaos I spied Micheline, seated on a high wooden stool, bare-shouldered, swathed in turquoise silks and glitter, blond hair floating about her head, angrily pointing a finger at Alan, who was down on one knee before her, looking up into her eyes imploringly.

"Forgive me, darling. Please forgive me. You're right, it was my fault."

"You know the woman doesn't speak English," she shot at him. "How could you do that to my mother? She's an old woman."

Anger with a French accent sounds more righteous than American.

His head went down. "I just forgot. Forgive me."

"She's sitting there in the hotel room waiting to be picked

up, and all the while you didn't send the car for her."

"I'll send it now. But, darling, it's almost time. . . . We have to go."

I thought before I vanished: Why didn't the daughter bring her mother?

A few moments later I was sitting in my seat in the last row, one in from the aisle, waiting for the lights to dim and the overture to start and for Alan to slip in beside me in the dark and whisper notes during the long performance.

After that night the scene was something like this: With two hours of script and production to cut, the score in a state of flux, Alan was still anxiously preoccupied with keeping Micheline busy and content (sending her flowers, providing her with zoo and museum schedules). It did not help that as the hours and hours of work went on well into the nights, Fritz began to back off and protect his health. At night, after the performance, he and Tammy retired to the hotel.

Alan's suite became a battleground. Nighttimes, after everybody had gone off to bed, Bud Widney and I, with Teddy snoozing, would settle into chairs, while Alan tried to tame this monster. In Fritz's absence Alan began to rely more heavily on Bud for story conferences. Fritz noticed. There began to be a hairline fracture in the precious crystal of Lerner and Loewe's collaboration.

Micheline's sleeping presence beyond the bedroom door kept our voices low. When it actually began to get light outside the window, and I had typed the new pages, Bud and I and Teddy would stagger off to bed.

Three hours later, when I was awake again and dressed, I would knock on Moss Hart's door.

"Come in," he'd call. In starched white shirt and tie, in the whitest undershorts, he was still the best-dressed man around. Not in the least flustered by his bare legs in garters and socks, he held out his hand and thanked me in the most friendly and elegant fashion for the new pages that he would have to wrestle with.

Bert and I were sitting in the hotel dining room in Toronto having dinner. He seemed to come from a fresh outer world that wasn't within my grasp.

So immersed was I in *Camelot* and its woes, so empathizing with Alan, that love in the afternoon with my darling was dulled and disappointing, although I pretended mightily to Bert that it wasn't. It was my fault.

When, getting up from bed, he said, "Let's go out and see the city," I begged off. Toronto to me was the theater and the hotel and a little park I took Teddy to. Its avenues and vistas would remain forever unknown to me. We ended up at rehearsal in the theater.

Now we were having dinner. Alan and some others were at a nearby table. He waved. He was looking crimped over his plate.

"I don't know how he's going to do it," I said to Bert.

He said, "Go to Alan tonight. He needs you." I wished he hadn't said that. I would have preferred an act of possession. I wanted another chance to be in his arms. But in retrospect, I think he would have had to ravish me at the table to pull me away from the show.

Bert flew off again the next day. As we kissed good-bye at the airport, I realized I was lonely.

One night, after Teddy and I had finished our dinner from room service in the hotel room, we went down the hall to Alan's as usual. The door was ajar. Voices were coming from the bedroom. As I went to the entrance, I saw Alan, dressed, lying on the bed, the hotel doctor standing over him.

"He's hemorrhaging," he said.

The next thing I knew, ambulance attendants arrived with a stretcher and in a minute had whisked him off to a hospital.

I knew what he was thinking. His father had had fifty-two cancer operations.

After a few days Bud came up to me at rehearsal and told me Alan wanted to see me. Micheline was there in the hospital room, like a bright bird. Wifely. Fixing his pillows. She was glad of the visit.

"Doris," she said, looking at him motheringly, "he's not allowed to work, but he insists."

Alan had better color after a few days' rest. He looked at me with apologetic humor, as if he'd spilled his grape juice on the white cloth. "Bleeding ulcer," he said.

"How do you feel?" I said affectionately.

"Feel fine. Did you bring the scripts?"

I gave him his and sat with mine. Micheline took a vase of flowers out of the room. I sat silently while he perused the pages. After a while he put the script down and said dejectedly, "I guess I'm too weak." Soon I was standing on the street in Toronto again.

It was up to Moss Hart now. And poor Fritz.

The next blow seemed unsurmountable.

A week later, as Alan was leaving the hospital, Moss Hart was wheeled in. Heart attack.

After my first shock I thought: Well, we'll just pack up this giant Middle Ages environment, with its high-altitude sets, dressy costumes, and the almost hundred people, and go home, just undo the whole thing, like a movie reel running backward until it goes down to the last frame and zero.

But that was fantasy. I learned that professionals don't give up.

For the first time Alan and Fritz had a disagreement. Among all the tangled discussions and rumors, I knew only that Fritz wanted to hire a new director right away, so that someone would be in charge at the theater while he and Alan were rewriting at the hotel. It made sense. Except I found out later that Alan had privately promised Moss Hart, through his wife, Kitty Carlisle, that he wouldn't replace him, that, he, Alan, would direct.

But Fritz felt his relationship with Alan was sacred; it was the two of them against the world. By becoming a director, Alan took a big step away from him. Fritz wasn't jealous; he wanted to keep the outside world from destroying their union. He couldn't.

To solve the dilemma, Alan made what he thought was a shrewd move: He hired Richard's father and mentor, Philip Burton, a tall, spare, academic-looking man, to come and work with the actors. It kept them busy and made them happy. Alan stayed away from the theater for a couple of days to let them get set. One morning we arrived to see what he had done. The actors were eager to show Lerner and Loewe. What appeared onstage was a sort of pseudoclassic, with all the energy and pacing for a musical that Moss Hart had masterfully induced gone.

We had no director. Alan had to take over. In spite of Fritz's objections, he stepped in as director. With Bud at his side and Philip Burton in the wings, he took the show through the end of Toronto, through Boston, and, with a week's postponement, into New York. Though Philip Burton's name appeared in the New York playbill as "Assistant to Moss Hart," I don't know if they ever met.

There was finally a last day at the enormous O'Keefe Theater, when they packed up the show and shipped it to Boston. On that morning, as we were leaving the theater lobby, Marlene Dietrich arrived with two young men at her side. Her one-woman show was moving in. Instead of looking eight years older than she had when she answered the door at Lillie's, she looked sixteen years younger. Amazing. She kissed and flirted with Alan.

*   *   *

In Boston we stayed at the Ritz Carlton. Fritz and Alan still had their sessions together because there was more music to write and adjust, but it wasn't like old times. Fritz, distressed, nevertheless continued to guard his health. He was no longer the full-time partner he'd always been.

This dereliction drove Alan further to Bud, provoking Fritz even more. It was one of the last stages of the breakup of Lerner and Loewe.

Despite the trouble with *Camelot* and the ailing Lerner and Loewe attachment, Fritz was always ready for a gag. One night in his hotel suite he disappeared into another room, leaving me with Tammy sitting on the bed. When he reappeared, he was wearing Tammy's nightgown, his big head and chin peeping mischievously out of a Peter Pan collar, his legs and feet bare. It was the last laugh we had.

One day Alan committed the worst breach of faith imaginable. In an effort to appease Micheline and keep her from leaving again, Alan told Fritz he was going to allow her to sit in on their sacred creative sessions. Stung, Fritz countered: If Micheline was going to join them, he would bring in Tammy as well. Hardly a solution for *Camelot*. I watched Fritz approach the breaking point.

One night the rift climaxed. I can remember cringing with Teddy on the bed in the Ritz Carlton Hotel as we listened to Fritz's all-night outburst of fury and pain down the hall. Luckily he didn't have another heart attack.

In fact, he wrote one more song. It was not handed to Julie Andrews until one day before the opening in New York: "Before I Gaze at You Again." Yet on opening night her performance was seamless.

The show was not a hit in the New York reviews. The sets and the costumes were. The actors were. The score was. But the reviews reflected the fact that the huge show lacked structure. The morning after the opening, Lerner and Loewe came

into the office with a businesslike set to their heads and said,
"We have to figure out how to put this show over financially."
They conferred with the company manager, publicity people,
financial advisers.

But the show was meant to find its way. Though top-heavy,
it had beautiful parts to it. One day Ed Sullivan, the master of
variety programs on television, invited the cast to perform
excerpts on his one-hour show. That's all that was needed.
From that night on there were lines at the box office, and
twenty-five years later *Camelot* still goes about the world from
time to time.

Camelot was the only show I ever heard of that went back
into rehearsal and rewriting three months after the New York
opening. Moss Hart appeared for the first time since he'd been
taken to the hospital in Toronto. He persuaded Alan to make
changes, and soon his master hand was molding the show into
its final shape. Box-office receipts kept rising.

Finally, *Camelot* was destined to have a place in American
history. Jacqueline Kennedy told of her husband listening to
the record of the last scene when he went to bed at night.

> Don't let it be forgot
> That once there was a spot
> For one brief shining moment
> That was known as "Camelot."

Ever since then, Camelot has been the theme of the
Kennedy years.

In 1961 Alan's divorce from Fritz was final. Alan wrote a
letter to him in Palm Springs, severing the tie. With rancor.
I never heard Alan get angry. He could be biting and nasty,
but in a soft voice. The night of Fritz's rage in the hotel in
Boston, I never heard Alan's raised voice. This letter was per-

haps his answer to that night. He didn't dictate it to me. According to Fritz, no one's eyes but his own ever witnessed the letter. He told me he put it in his safe-deposit box, and for all I know, it was still there when he died in March 1988. I wonder if he willed it to anyone. Alan knew how to break a relationship.

IV

Without Fritz, Alan needed a new collaborator. He went to the top and picked Richard Rodgers. Rodgers accepted. They looked for something to do.

This time Bud turned up with a loser. *The Big Love* was a book written by the mother of a provincial girl whom Errol Flynn took as his concubine in his last boozy days. When Bud read part of it in *Esquire* magazine, he believed it to be the underground classic they claimed it was, the subject being the desperate need people have to be near glamour and the lengths to which they will go to touch some of it. To show how wrong even geniuses can be, both Lerner and Rodgers were intrigued by the tacky story.

But that union was not blessed. They didn't have their hearts in it or in working with each other. Micheline complained about going for weekends to the Rodgerses' country house and being left with Mrs. Rodgers while the men worked.

I remember when Joey Heatherton was auditioned for the part of the girl in the Shubert Theater. She was cast, but now they had to find an Errol Flynn. How do you find *an* Errol Flynn when the whole point was that he was *the* Errol Flynn? They went to Robert Preston. He said, "You guys must be crazy; it's the most tasteless idea I've ever heard."

Alan started to be late and break dates. He was excellent at that, and I helped him.

Lerner and Rodgers never took to each other. There was no play or humor between them; it was like a business partnership. Richard Rodgers lacked the sweetness and wit and lustiness that Fritz Loewe had. To my relief, the play and the collaboration came to naught.

In 1961 we got a call from my brother, Howard, and I left Alan. I had to go. Our mother was dying of cancer.

Bert was working on *The Birth and Death of a Star* for public television. He couldn't come out right away. Bert said, "Why don't we take an apartment and move out once and for all?" Some of the things you do in life! We had absolutely no reason to move to Los Angeles.

I took an apartment. Bert came. My mother suffered and died. I was in shock over her suffering. Bert got jobs with the Army to make films in the desert. I stayed home with Teddy, rather than go with him and sit around a motel pool in the heat all day while he was out shooting.

There's nothing like the bright broad noon of a California day, with the papers read, with no one coming home that night, and the only sound someone hammering a fence. I took up knitting at Eva's Knitting Shop and knitted a whole dress with a jacket. Eva taught Teddy how to sit up and beg, but he missed his social life on the streets of New York.

When Alan called me back three times that year for short trips, I went. In between I think I was waiting for his calls.

Then one night on the phone Alan sprang me from my misery for good with the magic words "I have a new show! It's an original about a girl who goes to a hypnotist to stop smoking. And while she's in her trance, she regresses to the eighteenth century. Will you come?"

We'd already discovered that Bert needed to be in the East for his work, even though he would always travel a lot. He got a whole series on astronomy to do from New York.

We packed up our apartment and put everything in storage. I had a sad, bad moment about leaving the mountains and the sea, the sunshine, my father, and California life.

The Hotel 14 was on Sixtieth Street off Fifth Avenue, two blocks from Bergdorf's. With European overtones, baroque, carved, Oriental rugs on marble floors, it used to be a place where writers and character actors coming from Hollywood and Europe liked to stay, but when we pulled up in the car from California, we found it had turned into a residence for old ladies of some small means and assorted bachelors, though the Copacabana was still going strong downstairs.

Thinking it would be for only a year, Bert and I left our furniture in storage and took a one-bedroom furnished apartment there. I didn't mind the musty all-green rooms with the scratched furniture or the dirty windows. Bert didn't seem to either. I was as excited about Alan's new show as Bert was about his astronomy series.

Writing began in a festive mood. Alan was intrigued with extrasensory perception and even reincarnation. He had done some research, but I don't think it was profound.

On a Clear Day You Can See Forever was about a plain, unromantic girl who happens to be randomly bristling with ESP. In the course of hypnosis she emerges into another lifetime—another century, the eighteenth—as an enchanting woman. Eliza Doolittle backward.

Burton Lane, the composer, was a tall, gloomy, attractive man, who'd written lovely music for good shows. But the collaborative marriage of Lerner and Loewe was gone. Alan would still write a title to a song, and Burton would bring in the music for Alan to write lyrics to. But when they were in a room together, there was no electricity or laughs. If Alan missed Fritz, he didn't say so.

We worked in Alan's bedroom in the house on Seventy-first

Street. Later, as producer, Alan rented offices at the Waldorf.

Micheline was taking acting lessons. She would burst into the bedroom where we'd be working and tell us about acting class: pretending to be raped or to have an awakening. She still rode off with Tony in the Rolls to have her hair combed almost every morning.

Now and then she would give a luncheon in the Empire dining room that looked out on the formal backyard. At around ten to one on such a day, in the bedroom, Alan would tear off his shirt, go into the bathroom, freshen up, come out, choose a dress shirt, a tie, socks, shoes, and a hand-tailored suit. Alan was his tailor's delight, and they were his. When he walked, he held his head up, as though peering over a wall. His face was long and narrow, with a rather large jaw. He said he was one of the few men who could wear brown. He had lines across his forehead, which gave him a slightly anxious look, even when he was being comical.

Leaving me and the script in the mess we had created during the morning, he would rush off down the stairs to the luncheon. Afterward Micheline would come up to the bedroom and discuss the guests.

Despite the house, the son, and lots of servants, they didn't make much of a family life. Micheline ran a restless household. The servants were always fighting and being replaced.

Over the next three years Bert was away a lot. He went to Alaska for five weeks, to Europe, to Peru, all over the States, and to Israel. Alan would sometimes call me on an evening, and when I'd arrive, he would be waiting on his bed in the corner, saying Micheline had gone to a ball and he felt abandoned. I'm not sure whether she went out because he was working or whether he was working because she was going out. We would still be sitting when she came home, looking smashing in a Paris gown, disgusted by how boring stockbrokers were. In all truth, there was nothing much for her to do.

We were beginning to work till two or three o'clock in the morning, even when she didn't go to a ball.

One day Alan said to me in his offhand manner, which was a sign that he was going to say something important: "I've been seeing this doctor."

"What for?"

"I don't know. He gives me shots. He makes me feel good. And strange." He laughed.

"How, strange?"

"I can't describe it." He looked a little spooky.

He underplayed it, but in the next weeks he brought up Dr. Max Jacobsen's name from time to time. I had the grace to restrain my interest, but Alan had a new adventure, and I was intrigued.

Looking back, I realize that he wasn't about to experience these remarkable shots all by himself. He wanted company. I just had to wait. For about a month he mentioned the doctor in his most mysterious, seductive voice, with a nonchalant toss of his head.

Then, one day, I was struck by a sickening moment of dizziness. It passed, and I ignored it. But in the next few days it returned and settled into my system. Something was definitely wrong. Bert was away.

Our doctor recommended an ear specialist. I went. He said, "Your vertigo is caused by a middle ear infection. I'll give you some pills, but you'll have to be patient; it will take three or four weeks to clear up."

A few days later I was propped up in a chair in Alan's bedroom in the Seventy-first Street town house. My head felt like a balloon tossed in the wind, and I was nauseated. I'd never felt so sick. I wasn't even responding to Alan.

"I don't want to influence you," he said casually, looking up from his script, "but if you'd like to go see Dr. Max, I could arrange it."

"I accept," I said, without a missed beat.

"I'll pay," said Alan, reaching for the phone.

I took this naturally as a sign of his protection and largesse, along with his confiding manner of writing, my by now ample salary, his swimming pool, his Rolls-Royce.

The doctor's office told Alan to send me right over. It was winter, I remember, because I felt a punishing chill as I wove my way woozily one block to Seventy-second Street, crossed Park Avenue, and turned toward Third. I found the doctor's name on a private entrance door of a big apartment house, and I staggered through it into the waiting room. I was almost delirious with dizziness, but I was aware that about twelve people were sitting restlessly in the waiting room. I noticed Howard Cosell reading a worn-looking newspaper.

To my surprise, the beautiful European lady with her hair wrapped around her head at the desk knew who I was.

"Go in," she said, indicating the door behind her. "Go into a treatment room." The next day I found out she was Max's wife, Nina.

To try to describe the miracle, I have to say that I felt so sick, that despite the anxiety I felt going to a new doctor (will he take a chest X ray? I smoke; will he find something terribly wrong with me? Will he like me?) I lay down on the inviting plump treatment table and fell sound asleep.

I was awakened by a snarling voice and a fierce, angry figure of a large man looming above me.

"This is no place for sick people," he said in a heavy German accent.

He had a syringe in his hand. He put it on a table and pulled a tourniquet from his khaki pants and wrapped it tightly around my arm. I was so sick, even that felt good. No questions, no charts, no nurse. Just the syringe. He held my arm strongly and slid the needle into my vein without the pain of puncture. As I lay pinned to the table, I felt like an initiate in a temple. Our eyes met. I felt fluid begin to travel, carrying heat to my bare throat, to the deep cavity of my chest, my scalp. I lay in thrall, embarrassed, but slowly returning the doctor's smile, as the golden heat reached my stomach and radiated to my sexual core, flooded it, lingered a moment, and slowly receded down my arms and legs, leaving me through my fingertips and toes. I felt as if I'd been touched with the gift of life, as Michelangelo's Adam was by the hand of God.

Go describe the orgasm.

Nevertheless, I tried. "Well, that's—that's . . . the most extraordinary . . . I've never felt . . . never—never felt anything like—"

He cut me off. "Now go back to Alan. Eat. And don't talk too much."

I flew on the street. No longer cold. I was not only cured but filled to the brim with radiant, instant health, clear in the head as the sound of brass, joyful, in heaven actually. I felt this was what it must feel like to be an artist in the heat of creation.

Alan was waiting for me. "You look beautiful," he said.

I didn't fall asleep that night. I roamed and paced around the hotel apartment in a euphoria, forgetting to eat, until about four o'clock in the morning, when I fell on the bed and tossed for a few hours.

But my vertigo never came back; I threw away the pills.

I told Bert about the cure as soon as he got back. He snorted. "Stay away." Bert made science films with establishment giants and was suspicious of a sensational healing.

I said, "Come meet him. He really did the most extraordinary thing."

"No, I sure don't want to meet him."

Several months later I told Bert about watching a fresh burn on a patient's arm disappear before our eyes as the doctor slipped the needle out. Bert didn't want to hear about it.

As I think back on it, Alan inevitably started to take me

along when he went to the doctor. He also brought Micheline, who, after one sleepless night, refused to go again. But I craved another shot, even though there was nothing wrong with me. I got it.

Max was a big bear of a man in his sixties, with a head of still-black hair. German, vivid, wearing strong, heavy glasses, he would sit on his stool under the fluorescent light in the small treatment room and, with a syringe in his hand, study an array of vials on his counter. He would take calcium down lovingly and stick his needle into the rubber top. He would take other mysterious fluids and finally, with a sly smile, the little vial of Methedrine that awakened the body, increased imagery, lifted the spirit, and hastened the flow of creative juices.

"It's not for kicks," he would say. "Only for people who have work to do." Alan had work to do. The play was consuming more and more of his energies, and the tension in his life was building.

One morning a few weeks later I was sitting in Alan's room with my legs crossed and my chin in my hand, waiting for him to spring some lines. He was on the bed in the alcove, dressed in his Italian turtleneck, holding clipboard and Scripto pencil.

The sound of the shower from behind his bathroom door stopped. The door opened, and Micheline's head in a white turban popped out.

"Morning," she said.

"Morning," we answered.

In a good-natured scold she said, "Alain, you still owe me a Valentine's present, you know."

A present for Micheline required a trip to Cartier. He nodded.

As she disappeared into the bathroom, Alan looked at me and said softly, "I like to give presents voluntarily."

Uh-oh, I thought.

Later, dressed in a designer version of acting school clothes, she reappeared for her daily pocket cash. Alan reached in his pocket and peeled off three twenties.

"I'm late," she said, and off she went.

Alan put his clipboard down. He sighed. "It's sad," he said, "but familiarity brings a loss of luster."

I didn't speak at a time like this.

He went on: "Micheline's religion is getting too much." He gave me a long look.

"She's a devout narcissist, you know."

He finished with another sigh. "She's a woman who's been wearing perfume for too many years."

Bert said to me that night on the ice skating rink in the park, "The big love is going to end in a bang, not a whimper."

But nothing happened the next day.

The writing of *Clear Day* took three years and had many interruptions. When Warner Brothers filmed *My Fair Lady*, we took our scripts and went out to Hollywood. Alan had tried to convince Jack Warner to hire Julie Andrews, but he said she wasn't a movie star and chose Audrey Hepburn.

The national company of *Camelot* was under discussion. Bud Widney was going to direct.

One day the three of us—Alan, Bud, and I—were sitting around the pool at the Beverly Hills Hotel. Max Jacobsen's son, Tom, appeared to give Alan a shot of Max's nectar. We went up to Alan's room. I accepted an invitation to partake. Bud declined. When Alan was handed a phone, I was lying on the bed, arm outstretched. Someone was calling from Washington to ask Alan to produce a fund-raising birthday party for President Kennedy at the Waldorf-Astoria.

Alan was thrilled with the assignment. It was right up his alley. He knew exactly what to do.

He had been to Choate with John Kennedy, but at that time they were just two rich kids. They knew each other, but they formed no bond. By now, 1962 or early 1963, Alan's links to the magic tribe of the White House had strengthened. The name of *Camelot* had become identified with Kennedy's administration, and he'd been to dinner at the White House. Soon after he would form an intimate, romantic bond with one of the members of that tribe.

We went back to New York and put our *Clear Day* scripts away for the time being, while Alan got on the phone, his favorite instrument, to make the party. Everybody wanted to come. Burton Lane was just going to have to put up with the slowdown.

There was a rehearsal the day of the party. First we went to Dr. Max, and he gave me as well as Alan a shot. So high was I on the happiness shot that when we arrived at the Waldorf ballroom and I spotted Henry Fonda, I waltzed up to him and said, "Hello, Mr. Ferrer." He was outraged, almost agonized.

"Who do you think I am?" he wailed. In my state of delirium I felt only slight embarrassment. Later it became the most mortifying thing I ever did.

Audrey Hepburn arrived in her extraordinary sliced-thin elegance, her birdlike beauty. Leslie Uggams sang. Jimmy Durante, Ed Sullivan, Robert Preston, and, yes, Henry Fonda practiced their entrances and exits. Gay Talese covered the event for *The New York Times.*

That night Bert and I were trying to find the ballroom when suddenly a gang of men filling the space in a swift walk through a passageway came toward us. President Kennedy, tallest among them, was at the center, surrounded by protectors, looking part president, part victim, with Alan in a tux alongside him, short, solid, handsome. They charged past us, and I could feel the hustle and thrust of power in that moment.

For the finale Marilyn Monroe came out and sang "Happy Birthday to You."

*　*　*

Bert was right: Alan's fourth divorce ended in a bang. One day Micheline changed the locks on the doors of the Seventy-first Street house. Alan couldn't get in and had to go to the Tunisian Embassy next door and jump from its roof to his. Embarrassing.

Micheline picked the dreaded Roy Cohn for her divorce lawyer. Alan hired Louis Nizer. They went to court. Micheline took the stand in a dress with a demure white collar and a mischievous look in her eyes but the image dissolved when the judge suggested she might have purchased the one hundred pairs of gloves at the store recently to pad her high standard of living.

For several days Alan's picture was on the television evening news and in the papers. It caused Alan great distress. I can't remember why I was there in the court.

Close as I was, I never did know how the big lawyers worked out the settlement. Micheline was offered a certain percentage of Alan's profits from present and future shows, but she turned it down for cash. She didn't care to bet on his success.

And in the midst of all this, and against his lawyers' advice, Alan secretly bought himself a present—a dreamy house and pool in the woods on Centre Island, with grounds overlooking Long Island Sound. Had Micheline's lawyer found out about it, he would have tried to take it away from him. But Alan was determined to have it. He got it.

"Micheline doesn't want much," he said to me and the lawyers in the car one day coming home from the court. "She just wants what everybody else has." He paused. "All of it."

Micheline had to let Alan keep the house on Seventy-first Street, but she took Michael and went off to live in California. From there, through Alan's next four marriages, she periodically had to sue for late alimony payments. Alan didn't like to pay his debts, and even though he was still rich, he was spending great sums of money. When he died in 1986, he owed the government more than one million dollars.

Besides Centre Island, he had another secret. He was in love again. Even during the divorce proceedings the intimate bond that had developed from his Kennedy connection turned into a romance. She was a well-known married public lady, almost as prominent as Jacqueline Kennedy. For the purposes of this book, she will be called Frances Douglas.

Alan was divorced from Micheline, his fourth wife, in 1963. After a year of interruptions, and the assassination of President Kennedy, Alan had to address himself to his work. He was living alone in the city house. *On a Clear Day You Can See Forever* was already late. He wasn't ready to cast, but he wanted Barbara Harris for Daisy Gamble, Louis Jourdan for Dr. Marc Bruckner, and Gower Champion had already come to the house to talk about directing.

It was lonesome work writing this big musical, for which he had to invent everything, with no model to guide him and no Fritz Loewe. He sought diversion. In between writing sessions, we took daily trips in the Rolls with Tony to antique shops and designers' studios to buy things for the house on Centre Island. He had invited his lady love, Frances Douglas, to come there on a particular occasion. It was the kind of deadline he needed. One day we went out and found what looked like a large stage crew, putting the house in order. With everybody working overtime, the deadline was met, and the result was a homey version of an ideal serene, cozy country nest, where nothing bad could happen.

Meanwhile, 1964 slipped past, and *Clear Day* was postponed. The deadlines got deadlier, and Burton Lane was not the contributor to story conferences Fritz Loewe had been. Alan got a little rebellious sometimes and would disappear, leaving Bud to deal with a disturbed composer. Alan and I usually escaped to the house on Centre Island. By now we were visiting Dr. Max Jacobsen every day, a habit I was trying to conceal from Bert.

And then it was May 1965, and auditions were scheduled to start in a month. Bert and I were still living at the Hotel 14, Bert not liking it. At the moment he was in Israel, and I had already missed going with him to Peru, saying I couldn't leave Alan.

We'd lost Gower Champion, but Alan had gotten all the others he wanted: Barbara Harris, Louis Jourdan, Oliver Smith again for set design, and Bobby Lewis, the director of *Brigadoon.* Herbert Ross was the choreographer.

We had taken a suite of offices at the Waldorf for Alan to produce from.

It was Monday morning. Alan had promised everyone a completed script by Friday.

The script had a beginning, a middle, and three endings, but there were holes in between. Twelve or so songs were complete, but several more were needed. The song he was stuck on was "Melinda," which must make his eighteenth-century heroine real enough for Dr. Marc Bruckner, her hypnotist, to fall in love with her. Alan had been trying to write this song for three months. It had become his nemesis. Burton Lane, who had finished his part of it, was flipping.

It was not as if Alan weren't working on it. We'd been sitting up all night and all day and all night again. Dr. Max was helping us. I hadn't slept either Friday or Saturday night, nor had I taken more than a bite of the sandwich that Tina, Alan's maid, put in front of me. I was slimmer, and I liked it.

Now it was five o'clock in the morning of a strangely chilly Monday in May, not yet light. I was at home to bathe and change. I hadn't been to bed at all.

My phone rang. It was Alan, of course.

"Darling!"

"Me," I said.

"You left!"

"You were dozing. I slipped out."

"What time?"

"Around three."

"Did you sleep?"

"No. I can't sleep when I get a shot. I don't know how you do."

"What are you doing?" in that chummy, inviting tone, as if it were ten o'clock in the morning instead of dawn.

"I'm getting dressed," I said cheerily.

"How soon can you be here?"

"In a jiffy."

"Take a cab. And hurry, hurry." His voice beckoned in my ear, enticing me, promising me a day of meaning, of fun, and Max Jacobsen, whom I hadn't seen since midnight and needed to see as soon as possible.

Now at 5:05 A.M., I stroked black mascara hurriedly onto my lashes, gave a smile to the mirror, and grabbed my bag and Teddy, who was always ready to go.

Pierre, the butler, who answered the door in a cotton bathrobe, was hardly civil.

Alan Lerner didn't live quite alone in the house on Seventy-first Street, which was rumored to be up for sale since his divorce from Micheline. There was Simone, I think her name was, the large French cook, who prepared some of her newly careless French cooking to send up to the bedroom on trays. There was Tina, the young maid they had brought back from a French village a few years ago; Tony, the ubiquitous young chauffeur; and Pierre the butler, a slightly Mafia type, to whom an apologetic letter of dismissal was in the mail.

I slipped up the curving staircase in my high heels, with Teddy running ahead. I knocked and entered.

"Darling!" Alan always seemed genuinely glad to see me.

"Pull up a chair." He surveyed me with a slightly searching appreciation (a part of his charm). "Pretty dress." I smiled. Teddy made a little pass of greeting, but Alan turned to his clipboard and studied it as if it were a dangerous little animal.

"What's the name of a stone to rhyme with 'this'?"

"Amethyst?"

He gave me a quick little smile. "Thank you, dear." He wrote. I waited.

"Sit back." He sighed, passing his hand through his thick brown hair. "I'll have something for you in a minute."

Half an hour later he pushed the clipboard away, wearily stretched his arms and fingers to the ceiling, and groaned loudly. "If I can't write 'Melinda,' there's no show," he said softly, decisively. "No credibility."

"You will," I said, gathering up my script and bag and Teddy's leash as we headed for Max's.

"I can't. I can't."

Alan was lying on the doctor's treatment table. Max's office was not like any other doctor's office. For one thing, it was open at five-thirty in the morning. Under the fluorescent light a lady in a turquoise evening gown stood with her back and head against the wall. Two youngish men in evening dress flanked her. Tennessee Williams swiveled morosely back and forth on a black stool.

The doctor was holding a hypodermic needle and studying an array of varied-colored vials on the counter in front of him. There was blood on his polo shirt and sneakers.

"You mean you haven't done it yet is what you want to say," he thundered.

He took a vial down from the shelf marked "Meth" and stuck the needle into it.

"I mean I haven't done it yet," Alan said limply.

No one spoke.

"This time I don't think I can, Max."

We were holding hands, and I stood over him and watched the doctor while he mixed ingredients, like a cook. He ran a messy kitchen. There were broken hypodermic needles on the counter and on the floor; the wastebasket was overflowing with their wrappers.

"Auditions are a month away."

"You told me," said Max.

"Burton Lane has been threatening to quit again. . . ."

"He won't quit. He wants to write music."

"Friday morning I've promised everybody a completed script. Oliver Smith has to have it before he goes off with another show. If we have to postpone the opening in Boston again, we'll lose the theater. . . ."

"What else is new?"

"I've been coddling Barbara Harris for a year, and she's getting edgy about doing the part. We've lost Gower Champion. I had to fight to get them to take Bobby Lewis, and I'm going to have to nurse him all the way. . . . Should I go on?"

"If you insist."

"The costume designer has to have all the costumes on his drawing board within a week, and Herb Ross is waiting for the eighteenth-century scenes, plus I still have to lick this lyric." He reached for his clipboard with the notes, which I was holding on my lap, and held it up. "This lyric is killing me."

Stretched out on the doctor's table, he looked haggard and small behind his dark glasses. We were still holding hands. The doctor studied his shelf of vials and took down calcium, the heat giver. We watched the amber liquid trickle into the syringe and melt into the rest. Somebody knocked.

"Not now!"

The doctor turned to Alan, his eyeglasses magnifying his ferocious eyes.

"Do you want to work or don't you?" he said savagely.

"Yes, yes, I want to work."

"Then give me your arm."

Alan held out his arm. The doctor plunged a needle into his vein. Alan's eyes met mine in silence, and I could follow the journey of the heat throughout his body by the look in his eyes, which went heavenward and closed to receive the gift.

At length the doctor gently slid the needle out of Alan's vein.

"How do you feel?" The doctor's voice was thick with complicity, as he sat back on his swivel stool, surveying Alan like a bar mitzvah father.

"Whew!" Alan slowly sat up, awed and shamelessly happy, and rolled down his sleeve.

"Look at his face," the doctor said to me. "He looks twenty years younger." He reached for another syringe.

"I suppose you want one, too," he said grumpily, with his brooding back to me. We had been here just five hours ago.

"Here, darling, you lie down," Alan said, swinging his feet off the table and standing up in the shadowless light of the treatment room.

"Did you eat?" the doctor demanded of me, as I collapsed onto the table and stretched out.

"I tried to."

"Did you sleep?"

"I tried."

"How many nights have you been up?"

"Three, I think—since Friday."

"You'll give me a bad reputation," he said, angrily tearing off the wrapper of a syringe.

The fact was, we had seen Max three and four times a day since Friday. For us, Max was always there. The types of patients varied according to what time of night or day it was. For example, Wednesdays were MS days. A crowd of people in various stages of multiple sclerosis waited all day for the chance to be cured by Dr. Jacobsen. He never wrote up his work, so we don't know how much he helped them. I did see a letter from the well-known Dr. Harbeck Halsted praising Max's treatment of a patient's cancer, which had disappeared entirely.

The doctor had a weakness for theater folk and those in power and was as much involved with his family of patients as they were with him. Alan was his current favorite, and his deadline was close to Max's heart. He gave us direct entrance to the inner chambers through the back door, which opened the moment we announced ourselves. Rich patients like Alan paid for the poor ones, I gathered, and for his ample life-style, for he had now moved from Seventy-second Street to Eighty-third off Madison. Same drawn blinds, but a pricier location and large apartment upstairs.

There were mysteries. He would suddenly announce that he was flying to Australia or Africa (leaving instructions for our shots with his nurse, Anna). He implied there was a political element in these trips, that he was part of government. He showed us a photograph of himself with John Kennedy, Prince Radziwell and another man, all in chinos and polo shirts, taking a summer moment on a lawn.

One day Max told us he had gone to the Carlyle Hotel to treat President Kennedy himself who had come to speak at the UN and had lost his voice. It was Mark Shaw, the White House photographer, who had introduced Max to the Kennedys. Max quoted Kennedy as saying, "I don't care if you give me horse piss as long as I can speak." Max had to give the president a shot in the neck. After that there were mysterious day trips to the White House from time to time.

Max also had a picture of himself in Egypt on location with Cecil B. De Mille. "I was there to guard him against another heart attack."

He had rescued Eddie Fisher after his abandonment by

Elizabeth Taylor and had saved him from being what he called "a basket case." When Eddie Fisher had to go to Las Vegas to perform, Max's son, Tom, trained by his father, came to Eddie's dressing room in the casino and gave him his shots. Fisher, although cloven to Max, confided to Alan that he feared Max was giving us all drugs.

The Meth? The doctor himself was quite open about the Methedrine. By itself it was called speed. The dreaded speed. The kids who used it for thrills were handling a loaded gun. But prepared by the master, who combined it with his enzymes, vitamins, zinc, calcium, placenta, and other marvelous substances, it became the privileged treatment we had just experienced. We felt wonderful.

As we left that Monday morning in May 1965, with Alan stuck on the crucial "Melinda" and low in courage, Max clapped Alan on the arm and said, "Go home and work, and don't squander the gift." No one else was waiting to see the doctor except Tennessee Williams.

But Alan squandered it. Just as work was beginning to go well, a phone call from his secretary, Seth, told us he was an hour late, and that was the end of work.

When we got to our office at the Waldorf at ten-thirty, three men in shirt sleeves and a breezy, attractive brunette were drinking coffee from cartons and fussing with lights and camera. If the young woman felt any annoyance over Alan's lateness, it melted in the warmth of his apology. He had been working, true, and the time got away from him. She used it in the interview. It went something like this:

"Alan Jay Lerner." She smiled in introduction. "Famous lyricist, playwright, author of what has come to be known as the greatest musical ever written, *My Fair Lady*, inviting us to visit him in his own office from the heat of a deadline."

Sitting under the television lights at his own antique desk, he smiled at her from behind dark glasses into the camera.

"Stay," he had said to me. "Sit right there on the couch."

"Alan, what happens to your personal life when you're on a deadline?"

"You see for yourself what happens, Shirley. I forgot the time, and it got away from me, and I kept you people waiting. For which I'm truly sorry."

He could be disarmingly open, with nothing to hide. She loved him.

"The big news on Broadway this season is that Alan Jay Lerner is writing a new show: *On a Clear Day You Can See Forever*.

"That's right."

"This one is an original story. Could you tell us what it's about?"

"It's about reincarnation."

"Do you believe in people coming back from other lives?"

"Well, I've never experienced it, but I'd like to believe it."

He took off his dark glasses and exposed his eyes to all. His emotion could be seen in his eyebrows, which drew together and upward in a moment of confession.

"Only one life on earth is really a tragedy, Shirley, when you think that even if we live to be eighty, it's only a minute away."

He himself, I knew, would like to solve the problems of aging. At forty-four, he looked thirty-five, but he was having tooth troubles, and lately he was letting the barber touch up his hair on the sides.

Sensing a turn to depth in the interview, Shirley switched the subject.

"Alan, ten years ago, when *My Fair Lady* opened, Walter Kerr called it the greatest musical ever produced on Broadway."

Alan was looking at her forthrightly. Now he dropped his eyes.

"Do people often ask you what you can ever do to top that?"

He smiled openly and boyishly. "My mother asked me that on opening night." He shot a look at me. I shrugged sympathetically. "But I got over it." This made Shirley laugh, and Alan joined in.

"It must bother you a little, though, when someone asks you that." Like him or not like him, she was going for a good interview.

"No, it doesn't really," he lied. "Everything you do is a different challenge."

"And on this one you have a different composer: Burton Lane. After the brilliant years writing with Frederick Loewe, how does it feel to switch to a new collaborator?"

Alan was deft, but she was trying to corner him. I forget what charming thing he said to her, but he slipped out of her noose and now spoke easily about how he and Burton Lane worked together. Then she said, "Alan, how do you meet a deadline?"

He smiled sweetly. "I just meet it whatever way I can."

"Suppose you don't?"

He demurred.

"After all," she said, chuckling, "we're serious journalists here. Suppose you don't meet a deadline?"

"You don't don't." He looked at me. "That's what's called professionalism." I could feel a tight smile on my face.

"Auditions start in three weeks," he went on.

"Are you ready?" she asked insinuatingly.

"We will be," he said.

It was over. Four people followed us down the hotel corridor to the elevator, holding papers like petitions.

"I can't now," he said pleadingly. "I've got Burton Lane coming at two-thirty to hear the new lyric, which isn't written yet."

Back in the bedroom on Seventy-first Street, we were surrounded with yellow work papers, clothes tossed, sandwiches going bad, ashtrays filled. It was now about 1:00 P.M.

When the telephone rang, he grabbed for it like a swimmer surfacing. So far, I thought, his genius hasn't produced anything, but it will, it will.

"Sweetheart!" He shot a look at me. Whether it was to be sociable, or because he was by nature conspiratorial, whenever Alan was on the phone, he would converse in such a way that I could be an unseen part of the two-way conversation. It was Frances Douglas. His lady.

"You made a speech," he was saying indulgently, eyeing me. He melted, laughed, joked, invited. "You'd better come right over here where I can set my eyes on you." I thought: Another delay?

She was at LaGuardia. She would come by on her way home to the children.

Pierre, the butler, had obviously not gotten his letter yet, for he pressed No. 5 in the elevator for Mrs. Douglas, so that she could meet Alan in the penthouse. A little later he pressed No. 3 for Burton Lane to let him off at the music room.

I went down a flight from the bedroom to meet Burton.

"He's not here," Burton Lane said testily. He didn't sit down.

"He'll be here in a minute." I took his raincoat.

"Where does he go?" Exasperated. "I've been trying to reach him for two days."

"He was right here working till three o'clock this morning. I was with him."

"Did he finish?"

"He's close."

"He's been on that lyric for three months."

"It's a hard lyric to write. So much depends on it."

"Yip Harburg writes a lyric in twenty-four hours." There was almost hate in his voice.

I defended with feeling. "You know he'll be ready in time for the meeting."

"I don't know any such thing. Today is Monday. The meeting is Friday morning."

I allowed him to vent his rage on me, hoping to absorb some of it. It had become a part of my glamorous job.

He sat. "I thought when the divorce was over, he'd settle down and work. I was patient through all the court goings-on, the publicity, the lawyers' meetings. But nothing's changed. He'll never finish anything going to that doctor of his."

"That doctor has cured him of his headaches."

"That doctor will cure him of life if he doesn't watch out."

Burton Lane, sitting deep in the gold satin sofa, with his long legs crossed, fooled with a pillow peevishly.

"If he misses this deadline on Friday . . ."

"He won't miss it. You'll see."

I heard the elevator descending past the music-room floor. Burton Lane looked up suspiciously. The elevator lurched to a stop at the ground floor, and we heard the gate open. In a moment there were light footsteps running up the stairs, and Alan popped into the room, looking boyish, all apologies and friendly and ready to work.

"Sorry I kept you, old boy." To me: "Darling, would you run up and get my clipboard with the lyric on it?"

Alan all but put his arms around Burton Lane with enthusiasm as they went to the piano. From upstairs in the bedroom I could hear piano music. It was romantic music, too good to generate bad feelings. After half an hour Burton Lane closed the piano and went home, appeased for a day.

"How is he now?" I asked as Alan came into the bedroom and flopped down.

"Happier. Everybody's happier except me. I'm the one who has to finish the play by Friday."

* * *

"Are you all right?" Alan said to me. No. It had just turned Tuesday on the clock. He didn't look all right either.

We hadn't been to the doctor's for four or five hours, and we were both beginning to feel the familiar void in the chest, the great need, which only one of Max's shots would fill. But by tacit agreement, we denied it.

"Close your eyes," Alan said. "Take a nap."

But I couldn't take a nap. Though I felt a profound fatigue, when I closed my eyes and tried to sink into the realm of sleep, I was wildly awake down there. My heart was beating too fast. The doctor said not to worry about that, so I simply didn't. I had never experienced bodily failure and couldn't imagine it.

My mouth was dry. I sat with my eyes closed, trying for a deep breath, but when I thought of it, my lungs failed to give way and open, and I could take only shallow breaths. I opened my eyes to stop the panic. I longed for Alan to say, "Let's go."

"Let's go," he said. I never had to wait long. "Take your script."

He put on his moccasins and went into the bathroom and washed his face. We tiptoed down the stairs. It was 12:30 A.M.

"Pierre is still here," he whispered.

"I mailed the letter two days ago."

It was deserted on the street. A cool night. There were no lights in the apartment houses. People were sleeping in their beds around us. All we could hear was the sounds of our footsteps on the cold sidewalk.

We hailed a lone cab coming up Madison Avenue and raced up to Eighty-third Street as if it were open country, turned left, and stopped in front of the white brick apartment house, where, in the ground-floor window behind shuttered blinds there was light.

The inner office was warm and had the pungent smell of vitamins that Alan detested. There was a cluster of heads around the doctor, who was seated, hanging over his swivel stool, swaying and dozing at his counter under the light, with a syringe in his hand. The doctor looked ready to fall off the seat. He had been trying to find a vein in which to give himself a shot when he fell asleep.

"Max?" Alan spoke softly.

He woke up, smiled. He began searching out a vein in the top of his hand with the needle.

"There! There!" said someone.

He pushed the needle in a little, probing for the vein. Blood spouted, but the needle slipped out. He poked around for another vein. Everybody held his breath. The door opened silently, and a young actor, Felice Orlandi, came in. Felice was married to Alice Ghostly, the comedienne, and was helping Max. Now he was carrying a tray of vials of medicine that he had just mixed in the laboratory across the hall. Without disturbing Max, he quietly placed them on the shelf.

Alan waited. There was nothing to be done until Max had revived himself with a shot. He wouldn't let his nurse, Anna, do it for him. Anna, the beautiful, ravaged, tragic blond East European lady with sunken cheeks, who was Max's doormat, was discreetly tidying up the office. She must have been in love with the doctor for years. Max bullied her brutally though she was the only one he would allow to give him a shot. But not tonight.

The clock on the wall said one-thirty. We were just starting Tuesday. I'd been awake Friday, Saturday, Sunday, and now Monday nights. With Bert in Israel, I felt reckless and had some notion that it would be enlightening to see how long I could last without sleep. Alan would doze off from time to time and even sleep a few hours, but I could not. Every four or five hours, when the shots wore off, my body grew too agitated to sleep. The only thing to do was continue to get renewed by the shots, and somehow the dilemma would all work out. I was waiting nervously with Alan now for Max to finish waking himself up.

"There?" said someone, pointing. Max placed the needle, pushed a little. This time it went into the vein, taking the fluid from the syringe. There was a not quite audible sigh of relief in the room as Max's face began to show life. Nobody moved while he absorbed the experience.

At length he looked beatifically at Alan, who was sitting on a stool, writing on his clipboard.

"Well?"

"Not yet, Max. I have to keep going."

The doctor was already holding a syringe and studying his vials.

"You can work here if you want a change. Or go upstairs to the apartment."

So after we got our shots, we went into a treatment room and sat on the table with our legs dangling.

The problem with this song, "Melinda," was symptomatic of the whole show. How to make her believable? Melinda appears through Daisy Gamble's hypnosis and lives her tantalizing eighteenth-century English personality only through Daisy's lips. Yet Marc, the doctor-hypnotist, has begun to fall for her. The lyric begins, "It's just a dream, Melinda." She's a mere dream from this plain girl's imagination. Marc wants to believe in her, but he's a sensible man. How to make a song out of it? One of Alan's talents—an almost-in-love song?

Back at the house there were pages and pages of yellow work papers piled up during the last three months. I can't remember all the ideas Alan had for this song, but some of them were so silly that he wrote them in a tiny, tortured hand; he didn't want anyone to see. He kept probing and probing to find the answer.

Yesterday Bud Widney laughed and noted that Alan had

never spent so long writing a lyric, implying the shots didn't help. I denied it.

So he got "You're just a dream, Melinda . . . dealing me lies before my eyes, of days that never have been. . . ."

As we sat on Max's treatment table, Alan studied these words for a hundredth time.

"There's no Melinda. They say for sure—"

Suddenly Alan whispered into the room: "But don't go, Melinda!"

We looked at each other.

"That's it," I said. "For certain."

"But don't go, Melinda. . . ." We sat silently. At length he said, "What a wonder. I don't know whether I created it or discovered it."

The line released the rest of the song within a few minutes. The last line, "You and I know that long ago, before the dream, there was you," completed it. Now Marc could go on with his romantic pursuit of the eighteenth-century girl. The play could go on, too. It meant some rewriting, but that he could handle.

Flushed with success, a group of us went upstairs to Max's apartment. It was a big place with modern European furniture, some leather, and pillows. I remember Ronny Graham—the inspired, funny, troubled actor-writer-comedian—was there that night. Also Roscoe Lee Browne, the elegant and poetic actor. Neither was rich like Alan.

Alan went to the piano. In the early hours of Tuesday morning he played and sang "Melinda" softly, in his Fred Astaire type of classy, understated elegance and professionalism. It was Broadway show music at its best. It went right to the heart. It would go to the hands of the arrangers, who would color and enlarge and transform it for orchestra. It would be sung every night onstage in the play. With luck it would become a song on its own, outside the play, called a standard. Top performers would sing it in many styles on radio, on television, and in nightclubs. It would join the ranks of famous songs for years to come. And every time it was performed, Alan Lerner and Burton Lane would get paid for it by ASCAP. It was big business. It was why he was famous.

But for the moment he was trying it out on the doctor and the cluster of intimates and me, in the doctor's big living room in the early hours before daylight. Softly, tentatively, he sang it, with the reverence that accompanies a birth.

Later, on Tuesday afternoon, I can remember floating queasily through the lobby of our Hotel 14, past the desk and directly to the elevator. The doctor had finally grudgingly agreed to give me a shot to make me sleep. He hated to admit I needed it.

As we rode up, old Mrs. Wuthering was looking at my exhausted Teddy. In her high, old voice she said to me and a fifty-year-old cherub of a man, "The minister says that he is certain when we get to heaven, we will find dogs there."

At the tenth floor we emerged into the long, seedy corridor. I found a banana and a cinnamon bun in the refrigerator and sat down at the rickety wooden table and chewed on them in a dreamy way. I remembered to open a can for Teddy, but he sniffed and scorned it. I lingered, allowing my excited body to give in slowly to the promise of sleep.

When I finally slipped between the sheets and sank my head onto the pillows, the last thing I saw was the clock. It said six, but the blinds were drawn, and I had no idea whether it was morning or evening. I turned off the light.

When I felt myself beginning to wake up, I surfaced from a great depth. I did it lavishly, taking deep, quiet breaths and stretching along the length of my legs and into my stomach. Through half-opened eyes I saw dusty sunlight streaming in through the blinds.

I was lying in Bert's arms.

Aromatic in his sleep warmth, snuggled up to me, he lay with one leg pinning me possessively to the bed. Marriage!

My first thought was: He's safe from the skies.

Next, he's come two days too soon. It's Wednesday morning. What luck he didn't come yesterday. My body felt calm now. I must have slept fifteen hours.

Bert was sleeping so deeply he was hardly breathing. His closed eyelids gave him a look of innocence and provoked great tenderness in me.

"Sweetie," he mumbled, felt for me, and wrapped his arms around me tighter. He was delicious, with his smoky scent, his face rough from waiting so long at the Tel Aviv airport, his natural body heat high.

An hour later I was gazing at him in the bathroom mirror, touching him on the back of his neck, where his dark gold hair was beginning to curl. He took long, slow strokes with the razor up and down his cheeks. The bathroom was full of mist from his shower.

We were having a fresh start. The apartment had metamorphosed from a dump where I dropped my clothes to a home with a man and a woman in it.

It was 11:00 A.M. Wednesday. I was getting dressed to go to Alan's, but I wanted to stay with Bert.

"What time did the plane get in?"

"Two-thirty in the morning. We left five hours late. I'm glad I found you sleeping," he said. "You're not going to that doctor anymore, right?"

I had the pang of a narrow escape. At the same time I resented him a little. He wasn't paying attention. He hadn't noticed that I had tumbled from the first exotic incident into a three- and four-times-a-day habit.

"You're invited to meet him anytime," I said for the fifth or sixth time.

"I don't want to meet him. He's a Nazi."

As I felt the sting of Bert getting angry, I thought: After all, you went away to Israel. That's a form of abandonment. It was Alan who was waiting to embrace me with his clipboard and Scripto pencils when I came back from seeing you off at the airport. And now, five weeks later, you suddenly appear, and it's two days too soon, two days before the deadline, and my other life is supposed to stop. Then, with my usual mixed feelings, I realized Bert needed to be welcomed, while I needed to go to Alan. I got the brilliant insight that I could do both.

Bert came out of the bathroom. "I thought the play was finished," he said, starting to get dressed.

"It will be in two days. He has to hand out scripts to every-body on Friday. He can do it."

"You'd better go to Alan," Bert said, the same words he used in Toronto during *Camelot*. "He needs you."

I liked to watch him button his shirt.

"I feel like you're sending me away," I said.

"Well, that's what you want to do, isn't it, sweetie?" He seemed baffled.

"Yes." I sighed. "But I'll come home for dinner. I want to hear about your trip."

"I'll take you out." He flipped his tie over and made the knot.

"No. I want to cook."

V

The bells of St. James's were pounding noon when Bert dropped Teddy and me off in the car on his way to the lab with his reels of film. As I stepped out, there was sun warmth in the May air. The sky was very blue. Young mothers were pushing babies in carriages home from the park for lunch and naps. People were strolling on Madison Avenue. It seemed a long time since I'd been part of street life. I felt reluctant and slowed my steps before going to the front door. I had been away only since yesterday, but it seemed like weeks.

When I hit the bedroom, the deadline was still going on, as if I'd never been away. The blinds were drawn. Tina's cart and vacuum cleaner were waiting outside the room for the next time Alan would leave, so she could come in and make some truce with the chaos.

Alan was sitting up on his bed in the alcove, still in his pajamas.

"Well-l, don't you look glorious," he said. "You slept."

"Fifteen hours."

"Something else besides," he said, eyeing me. "A certain radiance. Bert is back."

"He came in the middle of the night."

"Like Santa Claus." Alan slipped some yellow pages from his clipboard. Offering them to me as a prize, he said, "I have something for you."

I looked. Act Two, a revised Scene Two. I brightened and went to the typewriter.

"I was waiting for you before I go to Max," he said, and got up and went to the shower. I decided then and there to refuse a shot. After my sleep and reunion with Bert, I felt nature being kind to me. I didn't need it. I wanted to be calm when I saw Bert at dinner.

"Pull up a chair," Alan called to me from the open bathroom doorway. With a towel wrapped around his middle, he began to shave.

It was my second shave of the morning.

"Bert really should have told you he was coming," Alan said, rinsing the razor.

"He did. He called from Israel. I just didn't pick up my messages until this morning.

"I hope you didn't tell him you were up for three days and nights." He looked at me in the mirror.

"No."

We stayed silent while Alan shaved his throat.

"Not that I think Bert wouldn't understand," I said.

"He wouldn't."

I watched him take choppy little hasty swipes at his cheek.

"Confess it, Doris," he said wickedly to me in the mirror, "it must have been a thrill to wake up and find Bert suddenly materialized in bed with you."

I pulled my chair out of the way as he lunged past me into the bedroom and his closet.

"It's really very romantic," I said, "for a man and a woman to live together, don't you think?" He was buttoning his shirt.

He stopped in front of me and grinned wistfully. "Doris, you're marvelous. Don't you know I'm the one who's been married four times?"

*   *   *

In the two days before Friday Alan had to write more eighteenth-century scenes, deal with the ending, and create the
lead-ins to all the songs. Those are the lines of dialogue out of
which the music arises and a song arrives. They require skill
and grace. The songs have to be planted deep in the material.
I knew Alan could do it if he'd work hard.

I typed a lot that Wednesday afternoon, while Alan sang
"Melinda" to Burton Lane, and I pulled myself away around
five-thirty. Needing to be all things, I went to the supermarket
and lugged home bags of groceries.

As any Hungarian housewife would be doing at dinnertime,
I was already cooking chicken paprika on an electric burner
when Bert came home at six-thirty.

"Sweetie!" His voice had a tenor ring. His greeting was
lately a little more hearty than what followed. But I felt virtu-
ous. If I was high, it wasn't from a shot. We kissed three times
at the stove, while he loosened his tie.

I poured us some bourbon, and we sipped together. But I
felt scared. Max's patients were forbidden to drink liquor. I
wondered, as I looked at the amber glass, if I would fall over
in a faint. But Roscoe Lee Browne had told me that now and
then he had a drink and it didn't hurt him. I hadn't had a shot
for a day and a half, so I took another sip.

"When will you get the film back from the lab?" I asked
Bert, as if we were starting a cozy evening at home.

Bert was walking across the room.

"The lab?" The door to the bathroom slammed.

I waited until he came out. "When can I see the film?"

He went to the television set, looking for news of Israel.

"Bert . . ." I realized he was still there.

"In a couple of days," he said. "We shot three, you know."

"When do I get to see them?" I went and put my arms
around him from behind. He gave my hand a swift little kiss.

"Soon," he said. Bert could be private like that, whereas Alan had to read anything new out loud.

I sat down on the couch next to him.

"You look good," he said, nodding. "Are you slimmer?"

"I think a little," I said, pleased.

"*Are* you going to that butcher?"

I don't know why I didn't leave it alone. But I knew I was going to get a shot tonight and stay up. I said, "He's really a sort of genius." Bert couldn't stand the word "genius."

He scowled and switched channels, but he said nothing. He turned up the volume. It was only local news. He turned it off, and I went to the stove. The silence that used to seem a sign of our closeness was beginning to feel alienating.

At dinner I listened while he told me about his trip. We ate. Bert loved Israel and felt protective. When he talked about it, he gave me the feeling he could save the whole country. That doesn't mean he wasn't subtle or hilariously sarcastic. As I looked at his handsome, tanned face, I wondered if he saw through me as clearly as he did through others. He wasn't saying.

I wanted to stay with him. I was already getting sleepy. But I'd promised to go to Alan. The dinner at home turned out to be only a visit.

When I got to the house at nine o'clock that Wednesday night, ready to work, the room was empty. By the time Alan burst in with apologies, late from his dinner with Irving Lazar at the 21 Club, I was restless and a little peeved.

"I can't go on working for you forever," I said. "It's a job. I have to make a career."

"You'll never do it," he flipped. "You know you have more fun with me than anybody else."

But Alan wouldn't or couldn't work. He couldn't gather concentration. Burton Lane called. Alan talked to him. Every now and then he'd doze off for a few minutes.

Max came. He didn't often go out, but he brought along a

blond millionaire and his girl, who took pictures of us in the music room while Alan was getting his shot. Just as it was finished, Frances Douglas called, and Alan asked her to stop by. Although nothing was said, Alan began collecting some of the vials that had spilled over onto the love seat and put them into Max's bag. Max grumbled about being hurried.

"G'night, Max," Alan said, and dashed out of the room.

I heard the elevator going past us in the music room as I was getting my treatment. Silently Max and his devotees packed up and crept down the stairs, the millionaire oblivious, saying happily at the door of his Mercedes-Benz, "A doctor a day keeps the apples away."

Back in the bedroom, I wondered why Alan was upstairs romancing Frances Douglas, while I, all hyped up from the fresh shot, was sitting alone with no work in sight. It crossed my mind that I was taking his deadline more seriously than he was.

It was too late to call Bert, who was probably sleeping off his jet lag. Besides, I didn't want to call attention to my absence.

What kept nudging my mind that Wednesday night when I was alone in Alan's bedroom was the feeling that *On a Clear Day You Can See Forever* and the reincarnation of Daisy Gamble into Melinda were becoming slightly tedious to me. If Alan had intended another Eliza Doolittle transformation in Daisy, it wasn't coming out in the script. And it was beginning to look as though the eighteenth-century scenes, which were the pretext for much of the production, were almost silly. I needed reassurance, and I dialed Lillie in California.

I knew it was Alan's call she was waiting for, ever since the other day when she phoned him and he aborted the conversation, saying he'd call her back. But I knew she'd be glad to hear from me in the meantime. She and Alex picked up simultaneously on the second ring. Alex hung up.

"Bert is back from Israel," I said to her mournfully.

Ever protective of Alan, she said, "Oh, I'm sure Bert will understand your late hours." She then told me in her luxuriant voice how meaningful it was to work for Alan, how glamorous, how pretty I was—each year more so—how valuable to Alan, how loved I was by Bert, how cherished by her, Lillie, as friend and as the only person who understood Alan and cared for him as well as she—even though she had been waiting by the phone for two days for him to call back. They had turned down a party at Lady Mendl's, she had missed her hairdresser for fear he'd call and find her out, and she'd hurried in her bath because she would be embarrassed to talk to him from the tub. In spite of all his selfishness, we both loved Alan unconditionally.

"The show is going to be wonderful," Lillie was saying.

"I know it is," I said, and thought: Of course, Lillie's right; Alan couldn't do anything really bad. He could inject class and charm into a walk across a room. And besides, who was I to have an opinion when such a big show in the works was in the hands of all the big shots?

"Oh, look who's just walking in," I said, brightening. "It's Bud Widney."

"I'll let you go," Lillie said. "Thank you for the call, Dotty. Better *don't* tell Alan we spoke." We both knew that Alan hated his friends to talk about him. We hung up.

Bud rolled into the room on his crepe soles, with his soft reddish beard and thinning hair, light blue eyes twinkling, looking fresh as a daisy. He was on the verge of losing his boyhood, as I was my girlhood, but neither of us knew it yet. He kissed me on the top of my head in a fatherly way, even though we were the same age.

"I came to see how you two are holding up," he said. "Where's Alan?"

"Upstairs with Frances-I-mean-Mrs.-Douglas."

Bud laughed. "Is that what he calls her?"

"When he's feeling feudal to me. To you, he calls her Frances."

Bud was still laughing. "He's such an impossible snob," he said.

"In a confidential moment he sometimes calls her Mrs.-Douglas-I-mean-Frances."

We heard the elevator going past us and landing on the ground floor.

"I'm here to sit it out with you two a little," Bud said, putting a match to his pipe.

Looking out the window, I saw Alan see Frances into the limousine. She had on an evening gown. The car pulled away and drove down the silent street.

"Maybe now he'll work," I said.

It was midnight. Alan joined us just as Thursday was beginning, and he and Bud and I took our scripts and went downstairs to sit in the big, bright kitchen. "For a change," Alan said.

The servants were sleeping. I said, "I'll make coffee." I went over to one of the black iron stoves that Micheline had imported from France and found the coffee. But I overdid it. The product was so strong it just sat in the cups and got cold.

"Go back and read out loud, will you, darling?" It was a new version of a scene.

I opened my script and started to read aloud in a somewhat clipped, articulated voice, phrasing for clarity, but without emotion, to indicate that I was not presuming to give a performance. After all, mine was the first voice to give back what he had dictated to me. I felt the responsibility of not decorating it. Looking back, I would say I took it all a little too seriously.

" 'On the other hand, if it's true that everything that's ever happened always was happening, is happening now, and always will be happening, then for all we know the Egyptians are right over there building their pyramids while we are here building our skyscrapers.' "

"Whew!" Bud said. "That's wild."

"Too wild?"

"I don't know." Bud hunched down into his kitchen chair. "I suppose you can get away with being pretty mystical these days."

Alan said, "The point is that when you look out into space and see the stars and the galaxy, you're really looking back into time; you're actually seeing the past—millions of years of it. Doesn't that fascinate you?" His voice got a little hoarse, and his eyes looked stricken. "Nobody wants to get old and die. None of us does. I don't ever want to die." His voice dropped to almost a whisper. "Do you? Do you?"

We nodded solemnly. I had never had such thoughts.

Two hours later, Thursday, around 2:00 A.M., we were walking through Max's waiting room. Bill Ball, the young director of the American Conservatory Theater, which later moved to San Francisco, was sitting at the desk in the semi-dark, working on a script. He didn't look up. Sam, the fruit and vegetable man, was unwrapping fruit to give to Max. His sleeve was rolled up, ready for Anna to give him his shot before he went down to the wholesale market.

When we reached the inner sanctum, we found Max had a full house. He sat with a beatific look on his face, basking in celebrities, as he filled one syringe after another.

Eddie Fisher was sitting on the treatment table, looking wizened and, like a small boy, gaping up at the dark height and breadth of Anthony Quinn. I gaped, too.

"What I really want," said Eddie Fisher, "is to be able to act like Tony Quinn."

Anthony Quinn was passing around drawings of dancers he had made at the ballet that night. Being the star of *Zorba the*

Greek and *La Strada* and a hundred other movies wasn't enough; he wanted to draw.

But when he saw Alan, he swooped down on him and buried him in an embrace.

"When this is all over, friend, and your show opens, I want you to come to my island. We'll swim in the Aegean. I have three houses: one for you; one for Max; one for me."

"That sounds better than life here on earth." Alan sighed and smiled. He lay down on the table.

Max smiled and nodded at his children showing family ties and prepared to give Alan his treatment.

I had in my purse the catalog of Howard's latest exhibit at the Santa Barbara Museum. I opened my bag and took it out and put it down on Max's counter. Tony Quinn saw it.

"Howard!" he said, taking it. "Howard Warshaw. Where'd you get this?"

"I'm his sister."

It was the first time I was being Howard's sister at Max's. I had brought him as close as I could into the warm, teeming room.

"I wish I could draw like that," said Tony Quinn in his husky voice.

He handed the catalog back to me. I again laid it on the counter. When Max finished with Alan, he swiveled his seat to it. I stood over him as he studied the pages. He took his time, examining the scope of Howard's embrace of both life and death. He pored over a drawing in which you could see every moment of a horse's life. At length he said, not looking up, "You can't buy that."

Into the room came Felice Orlandi, the young white-faced actor whom Max had trained. He brought trays of medicine, which he lined up on Max's counter.

At around four-thirty in the morning a small group left the office and took the elevator up to Max's apartment. Besides the doctor, there were Alan and I, Eddie Fisher, Bill Ball, and a man called Ralph, who did some mysterious work for the Sanitation Department. There had to be someone to make breakfast. I suspected Ralph was a garbageman.

Anthony Quinn had gone home around three.

Bill Ball was looking depressed and sat on a couch with a sad, vacant face.

"He'll be fine," said Max. He didn't say when.

Ralph went into the kitchen to make breakfast.

An African ambassador in robes joined us from somewhere. Alan said to me, "Play the 'Revolutionary Etude.'"

"Not tonight," I said, and instead went to help Ralph in the kitchen.

Max and the African ambassador went into the bedroom to talk something over. When breakfast was ready, they emerged, and Max was shaved, washed, and wearing a new black turtleneck sweater. The ambassador was smiling and regal.

We all went to the table, and Max urged me to eat an egg and a piece of bacon. I liked the sensation of not wanting to eat, but I tried to please him.

"Eat," said Max to Bill Ball. "You must eat."

It was beginning to grow light outside, but you couldn't tell yet what kind of day it was going to be. Our group gathered our belongings together and went downstairs to the office to get our second shots before the morning contingent of patients arrived. But already pacing in the corridor between treatment rooms was Hans Haffner, a wealthy young Dutch stockbroker, whose marriage to an older lady and fatherhood were only a thin disguise to his homosexuality. He came first thing every morning.

"Come," said Max.

Hans and Alan and I went into the treatment room. I was all but fainting. Alan was biting his nails.

"That's a nice silk shirt you have on," I said to Hans.

"I get them from my Hong Kong tailor. Fifteen dollars."
Hans looked smug.

I said something prophetic. "Is anyone keeping track of
what we buy from other countries and what they buy from us?"

It was 1965, before the Japanese had outclassed us. Max said,
"Pretty soon someone will come up to you and ask you if you
want to buy a cheap American." It wasn't only his shots that
attracted me; there was an echo of my brother's wit.

"Not finished with the play yet?" Hans said to Alan.

"Hold out your arm," Max commanded.

We were silent while Hans settled down and grew serene.
He smiled peacefully at the people in the room.

"Now go to work," Max said. "Have yourself a day."

Hans rolled down his sleeve and, putting on his jacket, said
benign good-byes to all.

"I unbitched him," said Max after the door closed.

"Now you," he said to us.

When Alan and I left the doctor's office at 6:00 A.M., we felt
swell again. Alan had Felice with him. Felice had learned from
Max how to give injections into the vein, and he would stay
with us so we didn't have to leave the house again that last day.
Almost good-looking, with black, curly hair, Felice was going
to audition for the show. Alan had promised to try to find a
part for him.

New York that early June morning was beautiful. The sun
was casting a rosy glow on the low iron fence around the privet
hedges in front of Max's office. The sky was a tender blue in
the clear, young day, and to me the white brick apartment
buildings with the sun on their tops looked like snowcapped
peaks, which reminded me with a pang of being with Bert in
Colorado in springtime.

We piled into Alan's little red Thunderbird and tore down
the street.

I had to get home before Bert woke up.

I remember, an hour later, out of the bath and in my robe, straightening out the back of Bert's shirt collar over his tie, taking a pair of scissors and clipping his curly sideburns and the hair at the neck, while we stood in front of the bathroom mirror together. Wrapping my arms around his waist from behind, I plastered my face into his back and smelled his freshly laundered shirt.

"Don't lose any more weight," he said.

If he knew that I hadn't been in bed the night before, he didn't say so. It looked like I was having the best of both worlds.

As soon as Bert left, I went back to Alan's house. The phone that day was as silent as a napping pussycat, but only because there was an army of people holding it at bay, waiting for Alan to release the final script for tomorrow's meeting.

The office had been standing by all week. The Copy-Fast Company was waiting to stencil and mimeograph the final copies and assemble them into twelve or more binders. Two secretaries were prepared to stay up all night, if necessary. And Linda, our receptionist, was in the office, ready to come up to the house and type from my rough pages. But now it was almost six, and she was probably combing her black hair and taking out her token to go home in the subway.

"Call the office," Alan said.

I dialed.

"Tell Linda that Tony will be down in ten minutes to bring her up." Alan was not going to meet this deadline quietly.

Linda was a small young, dark, sexy, tough, moralistic Jewish girl, not a bit impressed with Alan Jay Lerner, but young enough to have some of the pretty dew still left in her eyes. She had been working the switchboard and doing typing for a year. She was engaged to a dental student.

Alan felt challenged by her. He would sometimes try out an

idea on Linda to see if he could produce an emotion. He never succeeded. She was the only one in Alan's entourage who totally refused to be wrapped up in this adventure.

In the basement of the house was a little room with no window. It had been furnished as an office for Micheline's secretary, whose main work was to pay the servants, answer invitations, and spy on Alan. Now it was going to be used by Linda, whose part in this evening was to sit and wait and type.

She sat and waited for three hours and typed for one-half hour. Felice took the pages up and down the stairs.

At 10:00 P.M. Linda's fiancé came to pick her up and take her away. Linda put on her gloves, and they left the house like Mr. and Mrs. Young Dentist.

The shots Felice gave weren't any good. Alan would slip off to sleep for half an hour at a time. When my latest shot wore off, I was reduced to sitting like a statue, with my feet up on a footstool. Felice scanned Alan's bookshelves self-consciously and read. Finally, we went back to Max.

We were again up all night. I called the Copy-Fast people from Max's office at one point, but it wasn't until about eight o'clock on Friday morning that I could tell them Tony was on his way with the last material, and they had to get it back in two hours. "The meeting is at ten A.M.," I said.

I had decided to let well enough alone and not call Bert.

When the men arrived, Alan was in the bedroom with Max, Felice, and me.

"I'd like to seal up this room and walk away and never open it again." Alan sighed, holding out his arm.

"Don't be too hard on the room," said the doctor. "A play has come out of it."

"It's not a play yet, Max."

"It will be."

Tina had been instructed to show the men up to the penthouse. They were expensive men. When you think of the lawyers and contracts and letters and phone calls and lunches that went into bringing these people together at Alan Jay Lerner's town house that day, you realize it was a big deal. And they came, jaunty and festive, with all their craft and know-how, in their gorgeous knits and finely tailored fabrics, from high British to California tennis, as though they were coming for a weekend in the country.

Oliver Smith's hair had turned white since *My Fair Lady*, but his face was still that of a slightly wrinkled boy's. He had the usual young assistant with him, carrying the portfolio of drawings for the sets.

Burton Lane was affable among these people.

Tall, lanky Herbert Ross, the choreographer, was friendly to everyone, interested in everything, loaded with energy.

Bud Widney was owlishly jovial.

Bobby Lewis, the director, was a smallish, plump, enthusiastic man. He had been one of the leaders of the Group Theater and had directed Lerner and Loewe's *Brigadoon* successfully in 1947. He worked closely with Alan and would find himself working uncomfortably close to Herbert Ross.

The silver coffee service awaited them, with some of Simone's brioches and butter and jam. They helped themselves and stretched out on velvet sofas or strolled around the large, rich room, talking and joking, waiting for Alan.

Felice slipped down in the elevator with the doctor, and I slipped up the stairs and into the meeting behind Alan. The reason he was late was so he could look as he did: a man in his prime, fresh from sleep, shower, and razor. He was obviously the leader they had been waiting for.

"While we're waiting for the scripts, could we take a look at the sketches, Oliver?"

Oliver Smith's assistant, a tall, disdainful young man, untied the portfolio. They all sat on the edge of their chairs and looked at the set drawings spread out on the floor.

"I love it," said Alan. It was the rooftop garden, where Daisy Gamble talks to her many huge flowers.

"This would be where she sings 'Hurry, It's Lovely Up Here.' " said Herb Ross, studying the scene. He was beginning to choreograph.

"Right," said Alan. "And later they do 'Wait 'Til We're Sixty-Five.' "

They passed around three or four others.

"Nice," said Burton Lane, smiling in a melancholy way.

"I'm having a little trouble with the psychiatrist's study," said Oliver. "I'd like to do something nice, but I don't quite see it. I don't quite see him, actually," he said.

"Marc is an idealist," said Alan. "But he's no fool. He's a bachelor, a lover at heart, who hasn't found the true one. So he's developed this protective cynicism to hide his romantic needs. . . ."

"He sounds a bit like you, Alan," said Bobby Lewis mildly.

"Now I can't go on," said Alan, blushing. "I will anyway. I was going to say he's attractive. He's witty, or I hope he is. And I think, as played by Louis Jourdan, he should turn out to have charm. Louis has a lot of charm, don't you think?"

"Charm won't help him sing the songs," said Burton Lane, munching on a brioche. "Can he sing my songs?"

"I told you you've nothing to worry about, Burton. He'll sing the songs. And he'll remain in character besides. The way I see it," he said to Oliver, "Marc is a more or less idealized picture of what every man sees himself to be."

"I'll have to give it some more thought," said Oliver. "The script should help."

"Hasn't this classroom scene been scratched?" said Bud Widney. He was holding a drawing.

"Yes, that's right. Sorry about that, Oliver. I should have called you. We're not going to do that scene anymore."

They were poring over Freddy Wittop's costume drawings

when the elevator opened and Tony, the chauffeur, came out, holding the package of bound scripts. The finished show was beginning to emerge, and it was looking good.

Tony was definitely part of the adventure. He delivered the scripts as if he were bringing the Olympic torch.

"Tony," Alan said, "come over here and look at the costume sketches and the set drawings."

Tony eagerly knelt down on the floor with the others and shyly looked at the drawings.

"Now, this isn't the final version by any means," Alan said as Bud and I unwrapped the scripts and passed them out. "It's more or less a working script, but it won't hold up auditions; we can cast. It's too long, of course, but don't worry about that. I haven't licked the ending yet, as you'll see. That's what's held up the last three scenes. But we'll get all that down," he said, looking at me, "and have copies sent to you in the next few days."

So they went away, holding their promised scripts, with the last three scenes missing, but happy nevertheless by the excitement that the meeting had generated, and ready to go ahead.

Alan's movement toward the closet was quick. "I have a secret for you," he said.

"I won't tell anybody."

"You'd better not," he said from inside the closet. "We have enough on each other to hang us both. You can tell Bert, of course, because I know you will anyway."

He came out of the closet wearing slacks, with a pile of silk shirts and knits in his arms. I noticed his suitcase for the first time.

"Mrs.-Douglas-I-mean-Frances and I are flying to Venice for four days." He smirked. It was the kind of surprise he loved to pull.

"Venice, Italy?" Whew! I thought. Pretty risky. I knew she

had gone to the country house for overnight. But Italy! Certainly she, if not he, could easily be spotted by some reporter. Not wanting to say the obvious, I said lamely, "Aren't you exhausted?" The meeting with the men to give them the scripts was barely over.

"Max will fix me up with something to take along. Besides," he said with a happy sigh, "being with Frances is the most restful and fun thing I can think of. I deserve it, don't you think?"

I nodded.

He went to get socks and underwear.

"Here's a confidence. Only this one you can't even tell Bert." As if I wouldn't.

"It seems Frances has never been in love until now."

He said it with modesty, but a little smile at the corners of his mouth escaped. "With me. Would you believe it?"

"Oh, I don't know," I said. "You still have a bit of charm left."

"In public you would never think she could be so simple about love. So open."

She was just as simple, I thought, in her distaste for Max. Almost wifely. She even said something to me after Alan took her there one night and Max was wearing a white shirt and black tie for the occasion. She sat on a stool in his treatment room, regally, if that's possible on a stool, smiling gloriously while he told her he could make the whole U.S. Army more battleworthy with his magic shots, claiming that in energy, it would be like doubling the number of troops. I could see her smile turn to a slight, mocking sneer, and Max must have been smart enough to notice, or he wouldn't have gone to such lengths to make sure she hadn't seen him the other night when they both were in the house.

"Everything she does conveys a meaning," Alan was saying.

"No empty gestures." He chuckled. "Even her funny Freudian slips. We were walking down Madison Avenue one day, and as we passed the American Primitive Museum, she said to me, 'I just read that as the American Punitive Museum.'"

We laughed.

"She's a little taller than I am, but I couldn't care less."

I didn't know what to answer. The fact was, with Micheline, who was tiny, they had tended to look miniature, whereas with Frances, who was statuesque and athletic-looking, he seemed taller. Alan liked all types of women, I thought.

"You look good with her," I said. "I think I got you used to being with tall women," I ventured.

"It's true," he said generously.

The telephone rang. I picked it up. Burton Lane. Alan gestured no. It rang again. The office. "I can't talk now," he said. No business today.

It was two in the afternoon. He had other things to do. He had to produce this secret trip to Venice.

It's astonishing what a lot you could accomplish by just putting Doris on the phone. On Alan Jay Lerner's phone that is.

Within the hour the house was teeming with his people. His tailor, Sam Rosenthal, with new clothes that had been waiting just for his call; his barber, who came at once; a clerk from his lawyer's office with a paper to sign; someone from his accountant's office; his drugstore delivering fresh toiletries; his travel agent with airplane tickets. Alan was the only man I ever knew who could get a pedicure and look good while it was going on. By the time we left with Tony in the Rolls to go to Max's office, Alan was beginning to be late.

Whereas others might pack a picnic basket and a bottle of champagne and go up the road to the Hotel on the Mountain, Alan and Frances went out to the airport and got on a plane and flew to Venice. Of the four days, they would spend two traveling and had no time to get over their jet lag. Alan told me it rained. They failed to ride in a gondola—it was too damp on the canals to be inviting—but they strolled under an umbrella and paid a visit to the great square. Bert and I had been there one summer. I could see St. Mark's Cathedral rising like a dream, Oriental, ancient, the golden dome and the blue mosaic casting ghostly color through the mist.

They didn't run into anybody they knew, and nobody recognized them. Alan brought back a new gold cigarette lighter and two sweaters. But what he mostly came back with was news. Secret news. There was to be a yacht. He was going to charter a yacht to bring up to Boston in August while the show was there, so that Frances could come once or twice and stay overnight discreetly without running into everybody at the hotel. It would also be a good hideaway for Alan himself and for the doctor, when he came up.

But I'm getting ahead. While Alan was in Venice, I had a few days to catch up. Bert and I had the weekend together. We had dinner out, saw friends who had a baby, but I felt I was waiting; the excitement was elsewhere. And I missed going to Max's office.

That Monday at noon, a breezy, bright day in early June, I left our Hotel 14 and turned up Madison Avenue. I was going to spend money. In those days Madison Avenue was still affordable: nice small shops, pricey, but not yet international.

I needed clothes for my glamorous job. When I got in and out of the Rolls-Royce, people on the street usually stared. I had to look like a customer when we descended on the slick Battaglia Shop on Park Avenue, where Alan would go on a spree and pick eight or ten sweaters in white, yellow, red, blue, pink, black. I had to look like a customer at Sulka, where we went for the dress shirts and ties he would wear with the double-breasted suits Sam Rosenthal lovingly made for him, with colored silk linings, or in Bergdorf's antique department, where he once fell in love with a desk for thousands of dollars. "Get it," I said, without irony. "You deserve it." He labored so long and hard and lonely. I wanted him to have what he wanted.

I had to look like a diner when I went to the 21 Club to bring him his script or other papers and then depart. I had to look like a client when we went to Louis Nizer's office. I had to look like a first-class passenger flying to California with him. And soon I would have to look like one of a first-night audience in the theater in Boston, where I would sit next to Alan and take notes, then mingle with the crowd during intermission to hear what people were saying about *On a Clear Day You Can See Forever*.

Bert didn't want to know anything about my luxury shopping. Bert, who was openly generous, was strangely reticent about clothes. Once a year or so I'd coax him up to Sam Rosenthal's tailor shop on the second floor, and Bert would let us talk him into buying a jacket or two and some pants. Dressing for my job was a no-man's-land between us. We had developed a sort of tacit understanding that a new outfit would be fed unobtrusively into our lives, so that it would go unacknowledged forever. We were supposed to be living on his income.

Today, when I tried on a white dress and an emerald green sleeveless dress with a sassy little jacket I discovered that somewhere there was less of me. I had slimmed down from a ten to an eight. I'd always wanted to be pencil-thin. I knew it wouldn't last. After the show opened, there would be no more of Max's shots. I pushed this specter out of my mind. I'd face that when the time came. Meanwhile, I was on my merry, oblivious way to the brink of anorexia.

I moved on to the Italian shoe store, with its small Roman columns and Pompeian red walls. Wherever I went, I felt protected by the aura of money and privilege that Alan radiated, even in his absence.

"I have a few pair of special boots for next winter. A good price," said the Italian salesman, getting ready to wrap up the taupe pumps I had just bought.

"I can't wear boots," I said regretfully. "My calves bulge over the tops."

"Yes, you can," he said knowingly. He was a small, sinuous man with big brown eyes.

He brought me a tall, soft pair of black boots.

"Give me your foot."

He took my whole leg, as if he were holding a baby. "You can wear boots," he cooed. He zipped them up.

"They zip," I said, standing up and sauntering to the mirror. I definitely seemed to have slim, long legs.

"I love them," I said, a little shyly. "I've never been able to wear these before. I've lost weight."

When I left the store, I had two pairs of boots in two stylish shopping bags.

It was five o'clock in the afternoon. Sun still up. Daylight savings time. Something was missing. A thrust of yearning in my chest, a void in my stomach, but not for food, a cavernous thumping made me want to turn uptown to Eighty-third Street when I was expected five blocks downtown. The air was getting prematurely warm and muggy. I went home.

I put the two boxes of boots in the back of the closet and hung up the emerald and white dresses. Then I took my flowered cosmetic bag from the drawer into the bathroom. I removed a syringe and a vial of precious liquid. Finding the spot with blue marks on my hip, I closed my eyes and plunged the needle in.

It eased my tight heart and smoothed me down. But there was none of the traveling heat and instant new life that came only when Max's own needle entered the vein.

I heard Bert coming. He always turned the key in the lock at exactly six-thirty and came through the door in a celebratory way. "Sweetie," he said, and kissed me. He picked up Teddy, who was wiggly with joy and plastered his brown face against Bert's.

As we went into the living room, I saw the empty opened box with the tissue paper fluffed up. Bert pressed his lips together and frowned, took his newspaper, and went around me.

"Bert?"

He sat down in a chair and turned to the sports section. There was a certain alertness around the back of his neck.

I gathered the wrappings up. "What's the matter, Bert?"

Still looking at the paper, he said, "Look, Dotty, you're supposed to be putting your checks in the savings account."

"I do. Most of the time."

"We're supposed to be living on what I make."

"Don't worry, darling. You're going to make more. You're a filmmaker."

He looked up at me. There was trouble in his blue eyes. "Not those kinds of films. I probably won't make more than I'm making now—ever." He sighed, as if we'd been through it before. "Which I've told you we can live on very handsomely. Have our own apartment. Take trips even. But not for clothes, dammit."

"Okay. I'll just stay in bed all day," I said lightly, but I was fighting for my life. He was messing with my image of myself, trying to pull me out of my orbit. Marriage! It could be threatening.

"I mean, we don't have to live in a place like this," Bert said, passing his gaze around the musty all-green room.

"It's only a few months more until the show opens. And then my job will be finished."

This was the second time he complained.

"We've been living in a hotel for three years waiting for the

show to open. He's only writing a fucking musical, for chris-
sake. It's not as if he were inventing a cure for cancer!"

He was developing a nasty wit. I appreciated it, but it frightened me to see his angry eyebrows and furrowed forehead in
his long, narrow face. His mood felt deeply dangerous. I
wanted to make it up with him.

"I told Alan the other day that I'm quitting after the opening. I said I was going back to school." I didn't mention Alan's
reply.

I went over to Bert and tentatively stroked his longish sideburns. "Tomorrow I'll go look for an apartment." He took my
hand and kissed it. "But what if I find one?"

"Look for one."

Wednesday, when Alan got back from Venice, I was re-
freshed and ready to work, but instead of plunging into the
script, we paid a visit to the Waldorf offices for him to catch
up on paper work. This could be considered an amusement
compared with immersing himself again in *On a Clear Day*.

Alan's secretary, Seth Dansky, had a folder. It was called
jokingly by the staff Seth's folder. It stayed on top of her desk,
and she spent much of her time fretting over it, fussing with
its contents, rearranging the papers to reflect her version of
their importance. Those that had been in the folder for a year
found their limp way to the bottom of the pile, and there was
almost no hope that her boss, Alan, would ever take up the
matters of which they spoke.

Seth agonized over the neglected folder as it grew and
bulged, and Alan was amused by her moralizing. She was an
unmarried Jewish leftist from the old days, who had an apartment in Greenwich Village.

A poor junior high school teacher had been waiting for three
months for an answer about whether she could put on a scene
from *Camelot* at the school. Innocent enough request. Gordon

Dilworth, a wonderful guy who had played in two of Alan's
previous shows, wanted a job in the new one. He was in touch
with Bud Widney, but then so were hundreds of others. A
composer from Paris, who said he had a contract with Alan to
write a movie, was writing every week now to find out when
he could come to America for an appointment to discuss it.
The B'nai B'rith ladies wanted Alan to speak to them. I made
a bet he wouldn't do it. A college student from an Ivy League
school wanted to write. She was an admirer of Alan Jay Lerner
and looking for any small job in his theater world. I made a bet
that he would answer that letter. His first wife, Ruth, mother
of his daughter Susan, was in need of funds again. One of his
mother's doctors had a son who wanted to write. The Library
of Congress wanted an original copy of his new script when
it was ready. Ready? I thought. It's June now. Rehearsals start
at the end of next month. He hasn't touched the script for five
days. But Seth was going on about a charity ball, an interview,
an article, invitations to dinner parties, some already in the
past.

Seth had gotten to know every piece of paper in the folder
by a letterhead, a smudge, a turned-down corner, the color of
the ink. She dreaded the daily arrival of the mail, bringing
more letters to be sorted and placed in the folder, which was
always ready for the moment when Alan would call, "Bring
the folder!" Seth would grab her half glasses, her shorthand
notebook, and Scripto pencil and arrive in his office, small,
plump, with coiffed gray hair, hugging the folder in her arms.

Seth sat at the edge of a chair, her feet just touching the floor,
while Alan sifted through the letters at a table. Deep in the
goose down couch, I was watching. The door was open.

" 'Dear Ms. Brandford,' " he dictated. " 'You certainly have
my permission to put on Scene Three of *Camelot* in your
school. I'm sorry to be so late answering your request. All the
best.'

"There, do you feel better, dear?" he said to Seth, who was looking at him attentively as he went on to the next letter. "Write to Pierre Le Blanc, or whatever his name is, and tell him I'm out of town and won't be back for two weeks."

"I didn't know you were going to do a movie," I said.

"He's a composer friend of Max's. I said I would do a film with him." He sighed. "I don't know why. Or when."

"Let's answer Gordon Dilworth," he said, cheering up. " 'Dear Gordon: We'd love to have you along. It wouldn't feel right to have you missing from the new one. Bud Widney will be in touch.' "

He took his daughter's mother's letter and put it in his pocket. He accepted an invitation to a dinner party. And suddenly it was all over. "That's enough," he said, and handed the still-bulging folder, with all its requests for contributions, back to Seth, who took it with a shrug, doomed to carry her burden back to the desk again.

The papers in Seth's folder were fairly innocent. The big stuff went either to Irving Cohen, the lawyer, or Israel Katz, the accountant, both of whom had large staffs to cope. The bills, well, the bills, before they went to the accountant, languished in another folder, this one on the desk of Greg Kayne, who didn't agonize or give a damn, for that matter, whether Alan looked at them or not. The only bills that went directly to the accountant for immediate payment were Doctor Max's. Mine as well as Alan's.

The big issues for Alan Lerner, like could he buy the country house in Centre Island, must he sell the city house, when could he order a new Rolls-Royce, were decided over lunch at Pavillon with Israel Katz, who had enough friendship with, or influence anyway on, Alan to get him to drive up with me one rainy day to Westchester to address his wife's luncheon group of the local B'nai B'rith. The current letter from the Manhattan chapter must be fallout from the original event.

"Ask the boys if they'd like to come in now," Alan said in a friendly voice.

Greg came, skinny, show businessy, fancy. Bills were not all Greg did. He was a procurer. Procurer of fabrics for new houses and offices, last-minute theater tickets, items at auctions. It was he who got the good buy at the Parke-Bernet auction on the old French barometer that Micheline craved for their wall. It was he who took the train to the country house ahead of Alan and Frances Douglas to call off the carpenters that first day Alan took her there.

Wally Shuster. A quiet man, just starting a family, who later had a big office at MGM Records. He would induce artists to perform songs from the score. Even Lerner and Lane songs had to be navigated skillfully through the music world. He came in to hear the new one, "Melinda."

Bud Widney, his reddish beard neatly trimmed, had the casting folders.

They talked about auditions in two weeks and rehearsals a month after. I felt the excitement of the theater approaching.

When he finished with the boys, Alan said to me, "We'd better go."

To Seth he said, "Call Tony and tell him to have lunch and meet us at my mother's in an hour." To me he said, "I feel like walking."

Seth looked at him over her spectacles. "Where will Tony park the car?"

He delighted in unsettling Seth. "I don't care where he parks the car," he said. "The reason I hire Tony is so that I don't have to worry about where he parks the car."

I realized that Alan was dreading this walk up Park Avenue, which he tried to bring off as a stroll. We were going to his mother's bedside. He kept making funny cracks about the way Seth tried to make him feel guilty. If there was an ounce of guilt left in Alan, I knew only his mother could bring it to the surface. But where a chauffeur would park a car midday on Fifty-eighth Street and Park Avenue was not a question she would ask any more than he would.

She might, in her outrage, have boomed out to me on the telephone that if he didn't arrive in the next five minutes, she was calling off her cook and closing down the kitchen. She might remind him, as she had done all his life, of all the wounds she had suffered mainly from his father, who lived in another part of the city. She might ask a casual acquaintance if he thought her son was a homosexual.

She was large: large of girth, large of voice, largest of need. A consuming need for what must have begun in the early childhood of her heart as a need for love but had turned in the middle and old-age childhood of her heart to an all-devouring need for attention, from her doctors, foremost, and then her servants, her masseuse, her dog, and all her daughters-in-law. She had given up on her sons.

But she was dying now. Small stroke by small stroke. High above Park Avenue.

Ensconced in her large carved European bed, she lay swathed in bed linens, no longer, as Alan said, like the *Queen Mary* in dry dock, as the last stroke had reduced her to a loud whisper.

I sat by the bed. Alan stood. The room was darkened, but a thin shaft of sunlight slipped from under the shade onto the wall. Pearl, her nurse, was one of those incredibly kind and loving *religieuses* from the islands, who practice the care of others as they know God cares for them, whom one can, for mere money, hire to move into any household with their little suitcases and their expertise and take on the task that no one else will do.

"I love that woman," said Alan's mother in a strange hoarse, whispery voice.

Alan had a certain smile by which, in straining his eyebrows upward and twisting his mouth a little to one side, he conveyed a combined look of gratitude, modesty, love, longing. He smiled at Pearl in this way now.

"I had a dream," came Alan's mother's voice from the pillows. Pearl stroked her forehead. "I dreamed I went to a wake." She sighed. "Someone had died. It was a party. Everyone was there. And God came," she said, lying with her eyes closed. She opened them. "He wouldn't talk to any of us, but he was there."

"What did he look like?" said Alan, genuinely interested.

"He was a nice little man," she said, and sank deeper into her weakness after this expense of energy. She seemed very low to me.

Alan got up. He was restless. He roamed around the room. After years of callous behavior to his mother, he was shaken now. He left the room; I heard him on the telephone.

Alan's mother looked at me. "Is he crying?"

"No," I said, "because you're getting better."

When Alan reappeared, he said, "I have to go. You wait for Tony, and I'll meet you at Max's." He was out the door.

I stayed the rest of the hour, holding Edie Lerner's hand, while she fell asleep.

As I came out of her house, I saw a traffic cop approach Tony, who was triple-parked. I ducked in, and we drove off.

At Max's apartment house I went through the lobby to get to the back door. As I knocked, Felice Orlandi came out of the laboratory across the service hall. He looked haggard and wild.

"I haven't been to bed or eaten for five nights!"

"Gosh," I said. "Three was my limit."

"I can't leave here," he croaked hoarsely.

"What's the matter, Felice? Why can't you leave here?"

"They're waiting for me."

"Who is?"

"Can't you imagine?" he said ominously.

I couldn't imagine.

"They've got Max," he raved. "They've got him working for them."

I stared at him.

"Where do you think he gets all the money?" said Felice.

"From Alan," I said. "From Tony Quinn, Eddie Fisher, Franco Zeffirelli, Leonard Sillman, Tennessee Williams. Come on, Felice. . . ."

He brushed aside my answer. "They've got a billion-dollar business. And they've got Max to mastermind the supplying of it. And I help!" he said, with horror on his white face.

Standing in the corridor, I experienced a sudden, violent plunge into a foreign reality. What if? I thought. What if this whole embracing, pleasurable, delight-giving office were a mere front for a sinister worldwide operation in which Max, in his dedication to his medicine, was supplying addicts all over the country? I remembered the silent faces of strangers whom I would see in the shadows of the office from time to time. A moment ago I was thrillingly anticipating my first shot in five days.

"Where's Max?" I said. "I need to see Max."

Felice unlocked the hallway door. As we passed a treatment room, I saw my favorite opera star get up from the table and go to the mirror, a voluptuous, imperial, oceanic lady. I gasped. I hesitate to say her name, because memory might be teasing me. Bert and I had heard her sing *Tosca* at the Met. Max had hinted that he had an impressive new patient. He was going to help her sing better.

Felice is hallucinating, I thought.

"Felice, where is your wife?"

"She went out to get some sandwiches."

"Why don't you ask Max to give you a sleeping shot?"

He knocked on Max's door. "Doris is here."

Alan peeked out and said, "Could you excuse us for a minute, dear?"

Felice went in.

I felt rebuffed and waited in the airless hallway, wondering if the opera singer would emerge.

Presently Max and Alan and Felice came out of the room. "Don't worry," Max mumbled to me, "I've left instructions for Anna to give you your shot."

"And I'll meet you back at the house," said Alan.

They all exited together. On what mission? It was a rare event for Max to make an excursion in the middle of the day while a crowd of patients was waiting for him. They went out the back way. Where were they going?

"Anna, what's the matter with Felice?" I asked.

"He'll be better soon," she said. I didn't think she would tell me where they had gone.

Lying on the table, I watched the somnolent blonde in her white uniform and slightly run-down shoes prepare the syringe as delicately as one would handle gold flakes.

"Anna," I said softly, "tell me about the shots."

"What do you want to know?"

"Some people say they don't have the same effect if someone else gives them than if the doctor gives them."

"It's true the doctor has a special positive power."

"Are they habit-forming?"

"Life is habit-forming," said Anna.

"What is in them?"

"The doctor knows more about enzymes than anybody else," Anna said, holding the filled syringe in her hand. "He knows how each enzyme goes with the others and how together in different combinations they can work as catalysts to . . ."

I recognized the rest of the litany but never tired of hearing it again. Max was able to catalyze various wholesome and energizing life forces, to fill one's body with psychic as well as physical energy. More life. He gave you more life. Cicely Tyson was in the process of learning something particular about her creative powers. She told me as soon as she did, she would stop seeing Max.

Life was flooding me now as Anna and I gazed at each other.

"You look like a young girl," she said to me softly as my facial expression relaxed and deepened. "Beautiful." She pushed the last drop of liquid gently through the needle into my vein.

"The doctor likes you to lie down and relax for a few minutes before you go."

She quietly began picking up the mess that the doctor had left behind.

When I arrived at Alan's house, he was sitting on the bed with the pillows propped up and his clipboard lifeless at his side. He was wrecked.

"Poor Felice. We drove up to the hospital, and he didn't guess a thing. Until his wife appeared with the doctor. It was awful." He shuddered.

"He thinks some people are after him," I said.

"I know."

"He thinks they control Max."

"I know."

"He thinks Max is using dope."

"I know."

We looked at each other.

"I used to think that once," said Alan in an amused and offhand tone. "But it isn't true."

I nodded.

"Once in California I went for a week without a shot, and I was fine."

"How long do you think Felice will have to be in the hospital?" I asked.

"I don't know."

"Poor Alice."

"She had to commit him. That's the only way we could get him in."

"Listen," I said, "you can't think about this anymore. You have to forget it. You've got a show to write. You've just been away for four days, and now this."

But he only said, "First my mother, then Felice. I wonder what the third calamity is going to be today."

The third calamity happened about eleven o'clock that Wednesday, after Alan came home from having dinner with someone. He had changed into a sport shirt and slacks and was waiting for me to arrive back from my evening with Bert. I was a little late. I called.

"Where are you?"

"Coming. What's the matter?"

"Just come."

I found him curled up in the corner of his alcove bed, looking jolted. Max was sitting on a chair by the bed. Alan said, "I just got a call; I thought it was you."

"Who was it?"

"I think it was Robert Kennedy."

He looked so frightened that I tried to deny it with a flip remark. "Another birthday party?" I asked.

"No party." Alan looked at me. "He said he was calling to warn me."

"Uh-oh."

"He said, 'Listen, buster we've got a file on you. You're to stop seeing Mrs. Douglas.' "

"Holy smoke. The FBI."

" 'Or we'll fix your gondola,' he said."

"Venice!" I said.

Max was looking down at the floor.

"What are you going to do?" I asked.

"Marry her." He laughed a little nervously. "After all, this isn't *Anna Karenina.*"

Max said, "I'll get to the bottom of this threat business, don't you worry. I have my contacts," he added weightily. "There's a lot of power there, a lot of access."

"If it weren't for the crack about the gondola, I'd be inclined to think it was a hoax," said Alan.

"These guys are just trying to scare you," said Max.

"Well, yes. And they scare me."

As the world knows, Alan never did marry the lady we are calling Frances Douglas, although she went so far as to appear with him in Boston several times and at opening night in New York.

Alan's mother died quietly one day around that time. Typical of his understatement, he simply told me, as if it were a small event. I even thought he didn't care much, until Max said to me, "Stay with him tonight, he's suffering."

Fritz Loewe (*left*) and Alan Jay Lerner, creators of the movie *Gigi* and the Broadway hits *Brigadoon, Paint Your Wagon,* and *My Fair Lady,* discuss *Camelot,* their last show together.   BILLY ROSE THEATER COLLECTION; NEW YORK PUBLIC LIBRARY AT LINCOLN CENTER

Bert and I on our honeymoon in Malibu, two months after the opening of *My Fair Lady*

Barbara Harris and John Cullum in a scene from *On a Clear Day You Can See Forever,* the show that Burton Lane thought Alan would never finish

Dr. Max Jacobsen in front of the Colonial Theater in Boston. He had flown up to make sure that everyone got "vitamin" shots.

VI

It was late June now. Auditions were two weeks away. Rehearsals, four.

I could tell the script was nowhere near ready for production, let alone an audience. In the years with Alan I'd gathered enough know-how to realize that much. Alan worried that there was no production number early in the show. Marc, the psychiatrist, was still sketchy, though he had that charm. Alan was relying somewhat on Louis Jourdan. Eighteenth-century Melinda was coming through slightly wry, romantic, of course, and this was the voice she would use to tell of her tragic death in a storm at sea. Her alter ego, Daisy Gamble, the girl who goes to get hypnotized out of smoking, was charmingly awkward. In spite of the difficulties with Burton Lane, the songs were wonderful. But the script, though probably one third too long, had gaping holes. And there were still three possible endings.

Alan was nervous but said, "That's what we go on the road for." Remembering *Camelot,* I thought with dread: This show may not be finished until opening night in New York in October.

We were spending more time in our large, slightly worn offices in the Waldorf. During the days, when the staff was all there, people came and went. Bud was seeing performers; Alan had things to talk over with the company manager, the stage manager; Bobby Lewis would stop by. Excitement was building.

We walked with a purpose through the long hotel esplanades, where others were dallying, to the elevator, seeing out of the corners of our eyes the expectant travelers arriving and checking in with their luggage, bellhops at attention.

At night, when Alan and I and Teddy went to the silent and empty office, we would swiftly cross the block-long lobby filled with partygoers in the gowns you saw in *Vogue* and wondered where women wore them. At such times I always felt my life was more glamorous.

One night Max and his wife, Nina, came to the Waldorf offices. We were sitting around the large upholstered room while Max fussed with his bag, when suddenly Nina, poised beauty, with her luxurious auburn hair, said softly, "I don't feel well." Max heard her and began to prepare a syringe.

"No, Max," she said. "No more."

"Come," he said coddlingly. "I'll make you feel better." He took her into another room, holding the syringe. After they came out, she sat quietly, saying yes, thank you, she felt better.

About a week later, on the way to Max's in a cab one morning, Alan said to me, "Nina is dead."

"Dead!"

"Dead."

We looked at each other.

"What of?"

"Don't know," he said, and we continued to stare into each other's eyes. "She went to the hospital three days ago."

I have to look a long way back to remember how I felt. The detachment that came along with the shots slipped over the emotions so that the shock of this sudden death in Max's realm didn't fully penetrate, although the mind saw danger. Had he made an irreversible miscalculation when treating Nina? She died three days later in a hospital, out of his reach. Max had no hospital affiliations.

But obviously Alan wasn't frightened, for we went right on seeing Max. Behind the desk, Beatrice, chic, discreet, European, who was somehow linked with Max and Nina's life in Germany, continued to manage the needs of the many daytime patients. The office was thriving; sympathetic, but needy, faces surrounded him. I felt ashamed of my doubt and fear. And relieved.

A rush of pained sympathy for Max flooded me. I had a great need to comfort him and a dawning awareness that he was now an unmarried man. I had a traitorous thought. What if I took Nina's place? Forgetting Bert, I saw myself as a great man's wife, at the absolute center of the innermost circle. I already craved the touch of Max's hand on my arm. It seemed to me the underlying promise of his shots was an ultimate, awesome sexual act. Even if it killed you.

With these thoughts, I couldn't find words of condolence to say to Max, so I made a sign over my heart, and he nodded thank-you.

Everything went on exactly as if no one missed Nina's shadowy, lonesome presence in Max's ménage. Her death appeared to be a nonevent.

But an event that came closer to the heart of our lives followed. About a week later we found Max one morning in his bed, very sick and weak. He could hardly speak, but he managed to mumble, "That's the first time I ever took the wrong dose."

I was really frightened. Max had almost committed suicide.

Alan and I went several times a day to his bedside, where Anna, his nurse, would treat us, as Max lay like a beached whale. He could have been dying. I think we were the only patients he saw.

On the way downtown one day in the car, Alan said to me, "Don't worry. If anything happens to Max, I've got another doctor."

Another doctor! I thought: There are only a few geniuses every century. I imagine each of his patients worried about what would happen if Max died. He hadn't written up his work; he hadn't provided for his people. We were all dependent upon him personally.

I didn't want another doctor. Once I slipped away and went to see Max by myself. He was getting better. I held his hand. When Alan came in, he was annoyed. "I've been looking all over for you." I had overstepped. In some subtle way he conveyed to me that I was there only at his whim.

But it didn't alienate Alan. One night he said to me, "After this show opens, I have a new job for you."

I thought it was the opening line of a joke.

"You'll sort of represent me personally with the television people, newspapers, magazines, whatever. You'll be kind of the first stage of me."

He looked up at me, pleased. I thought: I'm going to get Lillie's job in New York. I didn't like the idea of change. Or being responsible for Alan's keeping promises and appointments. Doing sticky things for him. Like heading off the French movie composer. Even if it was in a good restaurant at lunch.

"It'll be a very feminine job," he said.

"I like to see you write," I said.

In spite of the pressures of the writing, Alan took a two-day trip to California shortly before auditions. I was getting tired of his excuses for not working. When he came back, he said with a voice of intrigue and a touch of rebellion: "I've brought someone with me." We were in his office. He went into another room and came back with a doelike girl, wearing a short-sleeved white angora sweater, slim powder blue skirt, high heels, with a little string of pearls around her throat. A California girl. Lisa was small-boned, white-faced, with black, lustrous hair combed simply and soft, wide eyes. A stewardess from the airplane. She was very quiet next to Alan and was already in love with him.

Lisa began sitting with us. "I'd appreciate anything you can tell me," she said. "I'm eager to learn."

In the beginning Alan sent her home with Bud at night, but within a couple of days she was coming with us to Max's for shots.

A few days later. I was waiting again for Alan to begin to work.

"Where's Alan?" It was Bud Widney in the office at the Waldorf.

"He's busy," I said.

"Where is he?"

"He's in the room next door with Lisa."

Bud started to laugh. "We gave up that room yesterday. It isn't ours anymore."

It was checking-in time.

"You mean, someone's liable to come around with luggage and keys and bellhop at any time?"

"That's right." He laughed.

I stood guard in the corridor, secretly hoping someone would come and partly amused in spite of my irritation. I watched the door open, and they came out, perfectly calm, happy.

"This isn't your room anymore," I couldn't resist saying.

Auditions at last. The first step into the theater. I had a love-hate feeling for auditions. I loved going into the theater and sitting in the dark with the creators of the show, though

I felt sorry for the actors. They are so vulnerable to the judgment of six or eight faceless people sitting in the dark watching as they come out onstage one by one to win shame or glory.

Even good professionals sometimes got passed over. The point was to assemble a cast that, put together, would make a company personality.

It was July. For several years actors, dancers, and singers had been writing in, calling up, and dropping by the office to see Bud Widney. He had a large collection of folders filled with photographs and résumés.

Bud had a weakness for actors, especially actresses and dancers, so he managed to span the chasm between management and cast. When he was with the cast, he had an old-fashioned lech for the girls, blended with a kind of lighthearted, youthful, romantic attraction that sprang from the pages of musical theater. But with his beard, when he was huddled with the writers and director and choreographer, with whom he had a colleague's status, he became a rather strict father to the cast in rehearsal and on the road.

The leads had been cast long ago. Barbara Harris was already a star among certain avant-garde playwrights and theater people off-Broadway. She had waited for a year and turned down other offers to make her ascent into Alan Jay Lerner musical theater stardom. She had told Alan her fears, her doubts, her feeling of hang-up because of the waiting. A shy girl in blue jeans, hiding within her the magnetic power of a star, she had come in the night to the house on Seventy-first Street. She had sat with Alan alone in the music room and been read to, soothed, persuaded, her excitement revived, her fears allayed.

Louis Jourdan was more assured. He was the star of *Gigi* after all. Urbane, charming, handsome, theater-wise, he could command the stage.

Now the rest of the show was ready to be cast. The psychiatrist's family. Five psychiatrists, including a mother. They provided the comedy. Then there was a secretary, Mrs. Hatch. There were the eighteenth-century British characters Daisy Gamble brought to life under hypnosis and her philandering husband, Edward (needed a pure tenor). Back in the present, there was the Greek self-made millionaire, who would rather have inherited his money than gotten it himself. And then there was Daisy's boyfriend, who wanted her to stop smoking so she'd fit into corporation life better. As I saw these readings onstage, I appreciated the rich mix of characters and material. I think Alan felt good about the play, too.

During this period we got shots from Max three and four times a day. I was trying to keep everything going, while hiding the shots from Bert. By this time he was helping by not asking questions, so that I never had to tell him an actual lie. I don't remember sleeping a whole night or eating a meal from the beginning of auditions through the run in Boston. That can't be possible, and I must have slept occasionally, but I can recall being up with Alan for nights and days and nights again at the offices at the Waldorf, and other nights lying next to Bert in the dark, terribly awake, pretending I was asleep, waiting for morning to come so I could go and get a relieving shot. The silence between Bert and me was crowded with threat. Even in my detached state I was aware that every evening he, a natural gallant, was sitting back and letting me lug home, unaided, huge bags of groceries. I would then cook, serve, and wash the dishes before I went back to Alan's at night. I became resentful. The fantasy of being married to Max that had come to me when Nina died returned once or twice. I began to wish Bert would go on a trip.

A few days later I got my wish. And another, besides. Bert went off to Washington to interview Dr. George B. Kistiakowsky, President Johnson's science adviser, and I had a visitor.

That afternoon Teddy and I stopped off at the Hotel 14 so I could bathe and change clothes. I also owed Teddy a run in the park. The silence in the apartment seemed intensified by the sound of the elevator going past in the hall. When Bert was there, the silence between us was alive with feeling; we were doing it together. This silence was my own, empty. It made me shudder.

In my hand were a few pieces of mail. A glance showed me they were bills. As I put them facedown on the table for Bert to deal with, a paper fluttered to the floor. It was a yellow telegram. From Maine. I read, "Dear Bert and Dot. Get ready to see yr. loving bro. Tuesday night. Luv from De Phantom."

Today was Tuesday! Teddy stared at me from his big brown eyes as I roamed around the room, laughing out loud at the image of Howard painstakingly communicating these spellings to the telegraph operator in Maine.

It was surprising how easy it suddenly was to tell Alan I couldn't come that night. I knew he could have Lisa.

But it wasn't until about ten o'clock that Howard called. I was pacing and needing some medication by then, but I couldn't go out until I heard from him.

"I'm at the Westbury," Howard said luxuriously over the phone. "Can you and Bert come over for a drink?"

To Howard a visit to New York was like the renewal of an old love affair. He was all mellow and healthy when he opened the door to me. In his crew-neck sweater and checked shirt, in the tenth-floor Westbury Hotel room, he looked like an exotic visitor; he exuded the mountains and the polo field and the ocean.

We kissed.

"Where's Bert?"

"He's in Washington for two days. Why didn't you tell us you were coming?"

"I didn't know."

"What were you doing in Maine?"

"I had to see the wall I'm painting at Bowdoin College next year. But I have to go home tomorrow." Howard got a lively look around the eyes, just as our father did whenever he was going to say something funny.

"You have perhaps heard of a man named Tillich?" he said.

"The theologian."

"Paul Tillich?"

"M'hm." I nodded.

"I'm going to sit on a panel with him at UCLA. When they asked me, I assumed it would be a discussion on painting and drawing, so I accepted. But I got a notice it's on 'Despair'!" A comical look on his face, he shrugged broadly and raised his big eyebrows, with his mouth agape.

"Why do they come to *me*?"

Over my laughter he was saying, "If you can come out for a few days, you can hear me speak on this subject."

"Oh, I wish I could," I said. "We're going into rehearsal. Working day and night."

"Why are you working day and night?"

"We just are," I said.

"Well, my dear sister, shall we go and have a drink," he said, "and celebrate our visit?"

I had another aim. I took a breath. "Listen," I said, trying to be casual, "would you come with me somewhere? There's someone I want you to meet."

"At this hour?"

"I want you to meet Dr. Jacobsen."

"Dotty . . . I know all about Dr. Jacobsen. I don't want to meet him."

"Just for a few minutes."

"Exactly what kind of a doctor is he anyway?"

"Please," I said, "just come." He agreed.

It was my dream to find Max alone. As we went through the

door of his office, I saw, uncomfortably, a few people slouching on sofas. I had to leave Howard there for a moment.

"Wait here," I said nervously.

I opened the door to Max's room. I got my dream. He was sitting on his stool, a little bloody and for the moment alone and subjecting his colored crystals to a certain light.

"I've brought my brother, Howard, to meet you," I announced.

He sat up straight, surveyed the mess of wrappers and needles on the floor and counter, and went for a white shirt hanging on a hanger.

"You shouldn't do that," he said, shocking me. Ever since he saw Howard's drawings, I knew he and Howard were bonded. Only the media they worked in were different. Max didn't speak as he buttoned his shirt, flipped on a black tie, and reached for a jacket.

"Come," he said rather roughly.

We went out to the waiting room, where Max rarely came. The two men stood in the low light. Howard was as big as Max, weighty, with black, untamed eyebrows and a ruddy Santa Barbara tan on his cheeks. He was the younger.

Max put out his hand, shook Howard's, and, to my amazement, muttered something like "I'm sorry, I'm late for an appointment. Another time perhaps." And he walked out the front door.

That was the whole meeting.

Howard and I walked to the Westbury Polo Bar in silence, found a booth, and ordered drinks. I hadn't had a shot since long ago that afternoon. I was running my finger around and around the rim of my glass.

In the soft, theatrically unbelieving voice of bewilderment that drove all but the best students at the university away, Howard sort of breathed, "*What* is a doctor's office doing open at eleven o'clock at night?"

I leaned in, took a sip, and launched into a description of Max's powers that Bert would never let me talk about, his cures, his everything. Howard had taken his white paper napkin and begun to draw a picture on it. I had a collection of such napkin pictures from bars. This one was becoming a comic, spooky imaginary animal.

I raved on about Max, getting shrill.

"And sleep!" I cried. "We don't need to sleep!" Shriller. "I don't think I've been to sleep for over a year!"

My brother, this man who confronted nature and tried to make meaning with only his brushes and paints, looked at me.

"What does Bert say about all this?"

"He won't come to meet Max. We're not doing too well together, to tell you the truth."

Howard handed me the drawing. "I love Bert," he said.

"I love him, too. But I didn't know he could be so tough."

Howard left me at the Hotel 14 that night, and I watched him walk up to Madison Avenue and disappear around the corner.

The next morning, as I all but ran through the lobby to go meet Alan at Max's, the doorman handed me a letter. It was in Howard's complicated, volatile handwriting:

Dear Dot. . . . First let me assure you of my perpetual concern and love. Has it occurred to you that you are living in an atmosphere of exaggerated crisis? The crisis is, I think, going on in you—and being projected onto daily situations. We have a family history, you know, of loopiness, what with Dad off to Florida for a nervous breakdown. [I had forgotten it; it happened when I was five and didn't impress me], Mother in the "rest home." [It was called civilized in those days for husbands to send their wives off for shock treatments for menopausal depression.] I, who totter perpetually on the brink—and now it seems to me you are going through a period which a nerve specialist might describe as moot. I'm hoping physical rest may do much to restore that balance of outlook, without which the machinery of reality turns unevenly. Life is essentially funny. Luv, H.

Nerve specialist! Rest! Howard could be smug. Superior. Popping into my life one night in the middle of a deadline, with auditions scheduled for today and the play not finished, and wanting to know why I'm working day and night. Time and distance have put us out of touch. Howard is in the spell of Santa Barbara and Academia.

Last night had been a flop. Forget it. I didn't need him *or* Bert to talk about Max with anymore. It was *my* problem. But not now, not now, not today. My nerves were bursting.

I waved a cab, praying he'd be a fast driver.

"Eighty-third and Madison, please," I said quickly.

A few hours later, on Max's nectar, feeling like myself again, I was sitting snug in my seat next to Alan in the theater.

A tough, rather cryptic young woman had just finished reading onstage.

"She gives me an idea," Alan said to the director. "Could we hear more?"

"Miss Allen," called Bobby Lewis. "Would you mind doing that last part again?"

The secretary in the play had not become a real character yet. This actress's reading had revealed something to Alan.

To me, he said in a low voice: "She reminds me of the kind of woman who, if you listen to what she says, you hear one thing, but if you observe the way she behaves, you get a totally different thing. That might be a funny angle for the secretary. I haven't known what to do with her actually."

Rae Allen got the job.

As we got in the car on the way home, I said, "I don't

understand what you mean." Lisa was tucked into the corner of the back seat. We had dropped off Burton Lane at his apartment.

"When my daughter Liza was born, we had a nurse who would say you can't pick up the baby every time she cries. Then the baby would cry and she'd head for the crib. 'What are you doing?' we'd ask. She'd hold and rock the baby and say indignantly, 'She's crying, isn't she?' Didn't you ever meet anyone like that?"

"I think Bert is a little like that."

"Emotional."

"How do you know that?"

"You just have to look at him."

I remembered that that was the word which got us engaged. I dropped the subject.

The auditions for dancers and singers were big. This show needed twenty of each, and some would double for minor parts. They had to be good. They would have to show off more training at auditions than they would probably be called on to perform if they got the job. Bud Widney had assembled fifty girl dancers. All ballet-trained. Energy galore.

I liked to watch them warming up in the wings. They were the people of the beauteous necks and shoulders, soon to be airborne. I liked to see them in their practice clothes, the leotards, the ballet shoes, a wisp of chiffon trailing at a waist.

Today was the choreographer's day. Herbert Ross was democratic about listening to everyone's opinions, but he wasn't about to give an inch on anyone he wanted or didn't want. Some of his favorites were in the audition today. If they didn't get twenty dancers out of this group, the producer would have to call an open audition. It would be announced in the paper. All would come. It would be a lot of trouble.

Singers came on another day. Tenors, baritones, sopranos.

When a baritone gets up and starts declaiming, "There once was a king . . ." you know you're in for many verses.

That day belonged to Burton Lane and Alan, both of whom cared how the songs were sung and if the lyrics could be heard. The director cared about a certain overall look for the show, like an artist painting a picture.

Max's shots weren't agreeing with Lisa. Within a month she had acquired the spooky look of a Charles Addams lady. I could handle them.

One morning I arrived at Alan's house on Seventy-first Street, which was quietly up for sale.

"See if you can help Lisa, will you?"

"Where is she?"

"In the bathroom."

I opened the door. Lisa was stretched out in the water in the bathtub, lying with her head propped up against the silk wall, the water up to her chin.

"Don't abandon me," she said.

She was beautiful, vulnerable, passive in the water, as if it were an element she couldn't rise from. I felt protective, and I was annoyed with Alan.

"I won't abandon you," I said.

Somewhere in all this I was becoming the older sister.

Frances Douglas didn't seem to feel endangered by Lisa. I don't know how those high society people work things out. Maybe she considered Lisa a lesser harem figure, not a rival. Perhaps Lisa was too young, not grand enough to be a threat.

One day Alan and I were supposed to drive up to Centre Island and hole up and finally settle the eighteenth-century part of the story. Rehearsals were looming.

To my surprise, Frances Douglas came in the car with us. I felt awkward on the drive out, as they were playing their own verbal games and laughing. You would have thought they were on vacation. I went for a swim in the pool, waiting for Alan to sit and work. But he and Frances went into the pool, too. It was a warm day. I felt wasted as I stretched out on a towel in the sun.

Tina prepared dinner in the oval dining room. Alan and Frances were clowning around at the dinner table. I felt angry that I was there. Then they went upstairs, and I could still hear them laughing.

Alan had promised to get to work several times that day, but hours later he hadn't. I was beginning to feel unattractively like a nag. If, as some say, there's always a woman behind a great man, I was reminded of Beethoven's imaginary wife when she was feather dusting in his studio and he cried, "I can't think of a melody. I can't think of a melody," and she said, "Don't worry, Beethoven, you will," and she hummed, "Hm, hm, hm, h-m-m-m," and said, "You will," and hummed, "Hm, hm, hm, h-m-m." And that's how he got the idea for his Fifth Symphony.

Soon they came down. "Aren't you going to work?" I said, with feeling. He brushed me off with some sort of good-natured sarcastic crack, and I heard myself saying, "One day I'm going to write a book about this show."

"Doris," Frances said, with a flicker of malevolent mirth in her gray eyes, "aren't you taking all this a little too much to heart?"

I should have paid attention.

The casting was complete. The company manager went to work. Contracts were drawn. People in high spirits were coming and going, signing, visiting, asking for scripts. Not yet. The scripts would be given out at the reading, which takes place the morning of the first day of rehearsal.

We were tied to Max by an invisible cord. Part of this time Bert and I were at a standoff. He had stopped commenting on my comings and goings. There was that silence.

Alan still had plenty of writing to do. As for the famous ending, he would have to decide which of three to use in time to get copies for the stage reading. He could always change one if it didn't work. He was writing inch by inch.

He complained, "I write myself out of one ditch into another."

Some nights he really tried. I had a rush of feeling for him. Alan did care, and in spite of all the fooling around and procrastinating, I knew he wouldn't give up. I believed in him.

What nagged him was that the show didn't behave like a regular musical. It seemed to be more a play with music than a musical. There was still no big production number in the early part of the show. There was no place for one.

I said, "You've made new laws before. The play goes beautifully. If there had been a reason for a production number, wouldn't you have seen it?"

"There is a reason," he said. "The audience expects it. Never mind. I'm not going to worry about it now."

We were sitting in his bedroom the next day. He said, "Is there a star or a planet or something cosmic to rhyme with 'lion'?"

Out of Lisa's mouth popped a little sound: "Orion?"

"Ah-h-h." He smiled.

"I didn't know I knew that," she said shyly.

Someone knocked.

"Come in."

Tina entered. Not quite as French as she used to be.

"What is it, Tina, dear?"

She handed him a note. Alan unfolded it. "Susan Savage?" he said. "Who's Susan Savage?"

"She's a college graduate who wrote you and wants to work for you," I said.

Alan, flirting with a diversion, said, "Should we stop for a minute to have her up?"

"It's up to—"

"Ask her to come up, Tina, please."

"Orion, eh? Let's see now. . . ." He studied his clipboard.

Now the above may not be the way Susan Savage actually became part of our entourage. The truth is, I don't remember. What I do recall is that somehow she got past all those people Alan hired to protect him from invasion, including me, who had been holding off Bobby Lewis, the director, if you please, for two days. Through luck or nerve, Susan Savage came to his bed-work-room at a time when he welcomed a reprieve. When I remembered the French composer who had a contract to do a movie with Alan and who, having failed for months to reach him on the phone, came to America, only to leave without seeing him, I marveled at the arrival of this girl.

She was the first yuppie I'd ever seen, long before the word was invented. Rather square-faced, with curly hair and bright eyes, her main claim to good looks was her youth. Someone must have told her she was beautiful, because she had a calm assurance, along with a dash of coltish audacity, which would turn to spoiled. She was oblivious of style.

"I hope you don't mind my ringing your bell," she said. "It was just irresistible. I can't believe it was so easy to see you. Right here while you're working."

I could see Alan relaxing and extending himself. He put his clipboard down and made ready to chat.

"You want to work on a Broadway show?"

"On an Alan Jay Lerner Broadway show."

"That's very nice. What do you want to do?"

"Anything." She sat with her mouth slightly open, waiting while Alan thought her over.

"Can you type?"

"Oh, yes. Mother is a writer, and she had me learn to type while I was still in high school. You can't go through law school unless you can type."

I watched an idea take shape in his head, and I could pretty well guess his trend of thought. This was no simple working girl. She came from a good family. She was educated. She was telling him that she planned to be a lawyer. What to do with her? You couldn't sit her downstairs in the basement to type, like Linda.

"What do you think about Susan giving Bud a little assistance?" he said to me.

I knew he had already decided. "I should think Bud would like that," I said.

"Maybe she could sort of float and help various people. Even us." He looked at Lisa. "That way," he said to Susan, "you could get a taste of various aspects of the production."

"Does that mean I could go on the road with you?"

He nodded his head slowly. "Yes. . . . I don't see why not."

She was going to enter this show at its most delicate time, when it was ready to rise from the printed page. The printed page that Alan had taken three years to write, in his bedroom, his various offices, his cars, his country house, Max's office. She would be a watcher, as I was, in the dark theater, in the soothing monotony of rehearsals, but she would never know the thrill as, stitch by well-known stitch, the play translated into a theatrical work onstage. Far from the private, intimate days and nights of writing words on paper, she joined us at the social, theatrical, festive moment when the actors, the stage managers, the sound men, the lighters, dancers, singers began their long journey.

So when Alan Lerner handed her a neatly typed and bound script, she didn't have a clue how it had come to be. One thing, if she were smart, she might notice there wasn't a lazy word in it.

It's not often we can make somebody completely happy. Parenting an infant probably is the only time in life when, with a mere touch of the warm little cheek or a cuddle, a person sometimes has the absolute power to provide everything another person needs for complete contentment. Alan loved to be able to do this. Looking at this young girl's face, he knew that he was doing it now.

She would start tomorrow. Meet us at the office at eleven o'clock.

We weren't at the office at eleven o'clock. Alan changed his mind. Instead, at eleven o'clock we were driving down the East River Drive, past Sutton Place, the United Nations Building, Bellevue. It was one of those leaden, sunless July days which, though hot, was colorless, as though the summer season had suspended itself. But we were coming from Max's and fresh shots, and we viewed the swirling gray river with dispassion. We didn't care.

At Twentieth Street Tony turned the Rolls onto a pier. We got out and walked the pier to the water's edge. A tanker filled the East River as it passed us. We stood looking at uninspiring Queens across the river, watching the sea gulls.

A bird in the sky came closer and got bigger and turned out to be a little airplane heading toward us, descending and getting louder, until it landed at our feet in the water with the motors running noisily. A small door opened, and the pilot reached out, smiling, yelling a hello, and took first Alan's hand, then mine, and helped us up into the little seaplane. He slammed the door and locked it, and in the din of the motors, we took off into the sky and rose above the river, flying parallel to the backed-up traffic, which Alan pointed to with satisfaction. It was too noisy to speak.

Suddenly we dropped and dropped and flew beneath a bridge, skimming the water. The first time that had happened, I was sure we were falling, but this time I knew we were dodging the jet lanes.

Out to the big Long Island, over houses, ball parks, schools in miniature, and beyond to the smaller islands, where the houses get bigger and the grasses grow greener.

We landed in water and stepped out onto a large, sloping lawn. Centre Island. Up the lawn and down a peaceful wooded country road to the white house with the curving driveway. Tina would come in the car with Tony in an hour's time.

Alan loved this house, with its own woods, swimming pool, and huge lawn of grass, with the water around it. The previous summer we had spent a lot of time there. Burton Lane had come out and worked with Alan at the piano, with the windows open and the sunshine pouring in. I loved to be out of the city in the country breezes.

But today seemed years later. Outside it was dull; the foliage looked almost gray.

"Isn't this nice?" Alan said. "Nobody can find us here." Except the doctor. A limousine and chauffeur were already ordered to wait at his office to bring him out.

Alan began to go through a ritual of getting ready to work. Scripto pencils, clean yellow paper, clipboard. Coffee, breath spray, nail file, cuticle scissors. Script.

"Shall we call Bud and see how he's making out with his assistant?"

Alan hadn't forgotten Susan after all.

"Sure."

"Buddy boy? What are you doing? What is Susan doing? I got her for you. But no nonsense. She's somebody's daughter."

They chatted, and Alan talked about the play with Bud. They talked for half an hour, and then he hung up. But he was restless. The work didn't go well.

It was gloomy looking out of the windows. Toward evening, when he had written very little he could use, we began to feel isolated, exiled.

"Call Max," he said at last. "See if he's left yet."

Extricating the doctor from his needy patients, his pals, could be an all-afternoon or -night affair. Max might plan to leave the office at four and get stuck until midnight, with one patient after another calling with a great need.

"If you can be here in five minutes," the secretary would be instructed to say. Embattled, embittered, the doctor would nevertheless continue to receive important patients, who would arrive out of breath all through the night. Having created the need, he might have felt he had no choice.

Only for Alan would he close up and leave.

Max was still in his office. I handed the receiver to Alan.

"Max? It's not working. Don't bother to come. I'm coming in. Send the limousine away."

Tina had set a beautiful table in the oval dining room.

"We can't disappoint her," Alan said.

We ate as quickly as we could.

"Let's go," Alan said. Tina would call for a taxi and take the train in when she had straightened up.

We needed our shots badly now. We had waited too long. Alan closed his eyes in the corner of the car. The country road was dark; there were evening lights aglow in the houses.

"How are you holding up, Tony? Are you getting tired?" I asked.

"Sometimes I get a little tired, but it's worth it. I feel privileged to be part of this venture of Mr. Lerner's." He slowed the car. "Do you know what happened?"

"No, what happened?"

"Mr. Lerner accepted an idea of mine for his script."

"Good. What is it?"

Tony slowed down to a crawl. I regretted asking him. If he'd put on some speed, we could make it to Max's in half an hour.

"It's words, actually: 'In the case of such a conclusive contingency.' The doctor's friend says it."

He had come to a boulevard stop, and although only two or three cars came past us along the dark highway, he stayed there parked at the end of the unlit country road while he talked. Alan was asleep, but I never understood how he could doze when I stayed so nervously awake.

"It happened the other night while he was waiting for you to come back," Tony said. "I was sitting in the kitchen when suddenly he called me up to his bedroom and read a whole scene to me."

"If you turn onto the highway and go fast, I'll ask you what scene."

"Oh. Sorry."

We were speeding smoothly. "What was the scene?"

"In the study. The doctor has just confided to his friend Conrad about Daisy Gamble's transformation under hypnosis. Is it true, Doris?"

"Is what true?"

"I mean, does she really reincarnate?"

"He thinks so, so maybe she does. I'm going to close my eyes, Tony," I said. "We have to work all night tonight."

When we finally got to the doctor's, he was unexpectedly alone. He had managed to empty his office so that he could be driven out to Alan's, and word hadn't gotten around yet that he was staying. He was sitting on his stool, radiating crystals. He was glad to see us.

Alan sighed and lay down on the table.

"What do you want to do?" Max turned to him and looked

at him in a fatherly way through his heavy horn-rimmed glasses.

"Work, I've got to work. I haven't done much today. It just didn't go."

"You'll work." He began to prepare a syringe. He seemed to be choosing more vials than usual.

"I want to ask you, Max, can you do anything for Louis Jourdan's voice? Burton Lane is worried about him singing the songs."

"But he was the star of *Gigi.*"

"Of course he was. But Burton is putting me under pressure. I guess he figures if the show is a flop, he wants good reviews for the score."

"I made John Kennedy talk; I can make the actor sing."

"I've told him about you, but I was thinking it might be good if I could drop by with him sometime when your big opera star is here."

Max stiffened. "This office is no longer for her," he said abruptly. "Her loss."

He paused with the syringe in the air. "You don't have to worry. I'll treat the actor. He'll sing."

He was approaching Alan with the needle. Alan hated the needle. But Max went right into the vein, cleanly, swiftly. He unstrapped the tourniquet. Alan closed his eyes and received the mixture with a deep sigh. Max pushed the plunger slowly, a little at a time. He looked at me; I returned the gaze.

"Next?" he said after he had withdrawn the needle from Alan's arm.

I was longing to lie down, but I sat. I knew Bert wasn't expecting me. He thought I was in the country. I was ready to lie to him if necessary. I put out my arm as Max approached me. Knee against knee, I sat with the doctor, face-to-face, my arm in the embrace of his warm hand. I supposed all his patients wanted to sleep with him. What about the men, though?

VII

The reading of the show took place on the stage on the morning of the first day of rehearsal. There had to be scripts for the entire company.

The night before the reading, Bud came with Susan Savage to stand by with Alan and me and Lisa and put the final touches on the script. Max came by sometime late. I thought of all the people around town getting ready for tomorrow.

"Anything you can tell me will be really appreciated," said Susan in an eager voice to me as we were going down the stairs to the music room.

"The script is already written," I said. I went to sit on the arm of the love seat that Alan was lying on. Bud was being supportive by just sitting on the piano bench looking relaxed.

"Well," said Max, "tomorrow you give birth."

Alan nodded a little grimly, but with a devil-may-care curl of his lip. "It's too late now."

"It's going to be great," I said.

Susan was watching, with her mouth crimped down in repulsion, as Max was sticking Alan in various places, blood spouting, and missing the vein.

"Max!" said Alan in pain.

Max finally connected. Everybody was silent as he got his shot.

"She, too?" said Max, indicating Susan.

"Not for me," Susan said with a contemptuous toss of her curly head.

Bud took Lisa and Susan off with him, and I stayed on with Alan. Nothing radical was going to be done to the script tonight. Changes, big and little, would have to be made on the road or in rehearsal. Alan puttered, fussed, made small adjustments. I typed a little; we sat, he dozed, we gossiped. It was more a ritual night watch than a working session.

When Bert opened his eyes the next morning, I was fresh out of the bath. He lay with his hands behind his head and studied me as I went to the closet, took out the emerald green dress and jacket and laid them on my unslept side of the bed.

"You haven't been to bed again," he said.

"I just came home to bathe and dress for the reading." My voice was chipper; I had had another shot around 6:00 A.M., and I wanted to go, go, go back to Alan's and ride to the theater, hear the actors, the piano, the songs in place, and experience this show come to life. I deserved it.

"You go to see that doctor every day now, don't you?" Bert said, not raising his voice.

"Certainly not," I said.

"I presume you know what it is you're doing."

"I went last night," I said. "Only because we were going to sit up, you know, because it was the last night before the reading."

"He's a Nazi," Bert said.

"He's a Jew. And he barely escaped the Nazis at the Berlin airport." I took cups and saucers down.

"He's still a Nazi."

But nothing he said could reach me. Until a few minutes ago I had managed not to have to lie to Bert. Technically. He helped me by his silence, but paradoxically I resented his allowing me to go off on my own and get away with it. I felt a momentary wave of despair, but I let it pass painfully through me and escape, without stopping to grasp it. Too late, I thought.

"Come have some coffee," I said, pouring it into the cups.

I joined Alan at the doctor's office, and we left for the theater from there, hurrying through the back door, for we had Max with us and there were patients sitting in the waiting room. It had started to rain, but we had only to step from the door to the car, and we never needed an umbrella.

The reading took place on the stage. All the speaking actors sat on chairs in a semicircle with their scripts on their laps. Facing them at tables, with their scripts before them, were the writer, composer, director, choreographer, and stage manager, Bud Widney, and, at his side, Susan Savage, the ambitious initiate, who had rushed in from the rain with her bundle of scripts from the mimeographer and handed them out to the company, as though she were bestowing presents. That used to be my job, and I was never very good at keeping track of scripts. My work was becoming vaguer, and I felt relieved. To the side of the stage was an upright piano. Dancers, singers, office people, assistants, wardrobe people, the producer, and the company manager walked and lounged at the sides of the stage.

The reading was a ritualistic event by which the writer was turning the play over to the actors. They were accepting it gingerly, tentatively, respectfully, as one tests the depth of unknown waters. They would immerse themselves slowly. They would inhabit their characters for a long time, God willing, and work together onstage eight times a week.

There was an air of festivity, celebration; everybody was eager to get along with everybody else; they were polite, good-humored; there were jokes.

At the moment, as the actors read their lines in thin, almost monotone voices, only the contours of the play emerged. But every now and then a big actory sound would escape from someone, a dry cackle, a wisp of humor, and there would be a flash of color. When a song came up, Burton Lane, sitting at the piano, and Alan, standing beside him, would play and sing it, bringing the script alive.

Barbara Harris, as Daisy Gamble, was hardly audible. But if you listened closely as she read her scene on the rooftop, some of the waifish, slightly comical, lovable quality that Alan had written came through and gave signs of the character of Daisy. Louis Jourdan's voice was familiarly French and elegant. He was the star.

It was two o'clock when they came to the last scene. After the final words were spoken, the whole company stood and applauded Lerner and Lane. The stage manager called a lunch break. Rehearsals would begin at three. Dancers in the lounge of the theater with Herbert Ross; singers in the main-floor lobby with the choral director; actors onstage with Bobby Lewis.

When Alan and I, and the doctor and Lisa, left through the lobby, Alan's play was in the hands of others.

Alan's next birthday would be his forty-fifth. It was going to come while we were in Boston, on August 31.

"What do you think we ought to do?" I asked Bud.

"I don't know if we should do anything," Bud said. "It's his forty-fifth, remember." I should have listened.

"It'd be a perfect time for a party onstage," I went on, "with all the company there singing 'Happy Birthday.'"

"He might like that," Bud said, puffing on his pipe. "I just wouldn't mention that it's his forty-fifth."

We had come to rehearsal to see a scene early in Act One. I was sitting with the doctor directly behind Alan.

Starting with the opening, in the psychiatrist's classroom, where he's lecturing about hypnosis, and Daisy goes under by remote control, we were reassured by the familiar lines being spoken. In Scene Two Daisy would sing her touching song to the flowers, "Hurry, It's Lovely Up Here." Barbara Harris stood in the middle of the stage, looking at her feet, waiting to begin. The pianist was at the piano. The dancers, in an assortment of practice clothes, were sprawled on the sides, some knitting.

"Are you ready, Barbara?" called Bobby Lewis from his seat.

She nodded. She looked like a schoolgirl. I heard the familiar monologue begin. Barbara was holding her script. The piano music slipped in.

The song came up. Barbara finished the lead-in speech, and the piano started to play. Suddenly, with a big breath, a big step, and throwing her script off to the side, she launched into the song with a belting, loud, rasping voice that would have made live flowers collapse. A big, showy number was under way. Thus was the character of Daisy Gamble transformed before our eyes! In the second scene of the play! She might never be recovered. Barbara Harris might never again be able to find her way back to the Daisy Gamble Alan had written. I squeezed Max's big hand in pain.

At the end of the number Barbara froze in place and looked expectantly at Lerner and Lane. Everybody applauded. Alan and Bobby Lewis left their seats and made their way up to the stage. Alan talked quietly to the choreographer and Barbara Harris, with his hand on her shoulder.

"They destroyed the scene," I said to the doctor.

"Don't talk about it to Alan," Max said. "He knows."

"But it changes everything."

"He knows."

"But they made a big production number out of a sweet, small song."

"Leave it alone," Max said. "Don't be a cow."

I laughed, and I never mentioned it to anyone else. The number was forever locked into the show. Without changing a word or a note, someone, I never found out who, had shifted the entire character of Daisy Gamble several degrees in another direction. And the direction was the shortest cut to the theater ticket office. Everybody liked it. The theater, after all, was collaborative.

The scene later turned out to be a howling success. It was praised by the critics. It was the production number that Alan had wanted and hadn't been able to write. The fact that Daisy Gamble had to come out of character to play the scene would be less confusing to the audience than a missing production number where one was expected.

Coming home in the car, we brought Louis Jourdan with us. He was handsome, had an actor's gallantry, and already knew all his lines. Though he was not a trained singer, he had been taking voice lessons for the show. He was going to half sing, half act the songs the way he did in *Gigi.*

"You'll sing, you'll see," said Dr. Max mysteriously.

"Okay with me," said Louis. "I'll try anything once."

The doctor didn't give him the big shot in his vein in his arm. He got the little one in his hip.

"How do you feel?" said Max gruffly, looking down at his hands.

Louis was a polite man. "Marvelous, Doctor, thank you," he said, tightening his belt.

"Let me hear you."

He let out a note.

"Can you hear your voice in your ears?"

Louis sang a phrase. "Yes, I can. Like an echo chamber?"

Max nodded wisely. "Now go back and tell me how you sing."

*   *   *

"I hope you don't mind," Alan said one morning when I arrived. "I told Susan she could sit in with us for a little while. She's so eager to learn, she made it hard for me to refuse her."

"Aren't we going to the theater?"

"This afternoon. I decided to stay home this morning and work on the lyric."

Soon there was a knock on the door, and Susan, with her freshly scrubbed look, walked in.

"Good morning," she said, almost welcoming us. She sat down and took out her new clipboard.

"All right now, hush, girls," Alan said, and began to think. "What's a state of mind to rhyme with 'I don't care'?"

I thought. "Despair?"

"No, I don't want to use that."

We all thought.

"How about a United State—like Delaware?" said Susan.

"No, dear, thank you, you're cute, but it has to be a state of mind." Alan was suppressing his annoyance.

"Disrepair?" I said.

"H-mmm." He began to write, keeping his clipboard close so we wouldn't see the words.

"That might just work," he said without looking up. "Sit there."

Alan was crossing the room. We were alone. He had a plaintive look on his face.

"I'm trying to get away for a few hours to take Frances to see the yacht. Darling, maybe you could stay here and head off the phone." He poked his head out of the closet. "Would you do that for me? Don't tell a soul where I am. Not even Bud if he calls. I don't want anybody to know about the yacht. That means anybody," he said emphatically. "Except Bert, of course. He knows already."

Alan's secrets usually had a limited life expectancy. Planted

in the intimacy of a two-way conversation in the privacy of a
room, a secret was buried deep. When first one and then
another of his people would start looking cryptic, and finally
when no one was talking to anybody else in the office, it would
turn out they all were carrying the same secret.

The yacht was created as a trysting place for Alan and
Frances Douglas, but so far she was only going to travel up
with him on the sea from New York to Boston, stay overnight,
and fly home. She might come up one more time. It had
already occurred to Alan the yacht would be a good place for
him to escape from the hotel if the going got rough. And if Max
and his paraphernalia became a problem, he, too, could stay on
the boat. Just not when Frances Douglas came.

"Where's Alan?" It was Burton Lane in the darkened
theater.

"He's coming." Me, still being protective.

Louis Jourdan was singing onstage to the piano.

"Have you noticed," I said, "his voice seems to sound
bigger?"

"I'm still worried," Burton said to Bud.

"He sounds like the character to me," Bud said. "A little
biting, impatient, almost bullying when it comes to the establishment. I don't think Alan intended him to stand still and
sing a song."

"He may be all right in the patter songs, but he's going to
need a voice for 'On a Clear Day.'"

"Do you notice," said Alan's voice in the dark—he slipped
into a seat—"how his voice is improved?"

"He's not a singer, Alan."

"But listen to him. Don't you notice a change?"

"He's a sweet guy and a good actor, but I'm worried about
him singing my score."

"Well, don't. He'll do it. He's a star, you know."

Herbert Ross and Bobby Lewis were having a discussion onstage. Herb Ross was winning. Bobby Lewis was giving way. Alan was letting it happen.

It was hard to leave the soporific monotony of rehearsals in the theater and go out into Times Square daylight. We left from the front door, through the lobby. Sometimes Alan was recognized. Sometimes he was asked for an autograph. Usually he was with an entourage. Today it was only me. We went toward the gleaming Rolls-Royce. When Tony saw us, he hopped out and stood by the open door, chauffeur-style.

"Some people get to ride in Rolls-Royces," sneered a bum-type guy, suddenly pushing his face up to Alan's.

"Listen, buster, I work harder in one week than you worked all your life," said Alan, with gritted teeth, getting in, me behind. In a minute a crowd would have formed.

We were going to rehearsals every day now. There were new scenes to look at, costumes, dances, vocal choruses. We were getting ready for the first run-through. For the first time Alan could stand back a little and let others prepare.

Alan didn't like being unmarried. He hated living alone. He was by choice a married man. At his happiest he was newly married. The fact that he had had four different families and each time got a fresh new wife and a fresh new house, or houses, didn't change his innate craving for a family, the lights of home, and all that. And he truly loved his four children. From a practical point of view, however, it was better to be unmarried when he was on a deadline. With me as his constant work companion, and now Lisa Echols, who was in love with him and turned out to be quite bright and no problem, and Susan Savage, who would become an integral part of his life, plus the whole company in rehearsal, he had enough to relieve him from the tedium of playwriting, and was for the moment safe.

Frances Douglas was still around but appeared only intermittently at rehearsals, preferring to visit Alan at night in the city house, never at the Waldorf office and never again at Max's.

It was 1:00 A.M. one night shortly before the show went to Boston. I was dialing Alan from a pay phone.

"It's Doris," I said.

"Where are you?"

"At the IBM computer center."

"What are you doing?"

"Not much. Watching Bert direct a film."

"Do you want to stay there?"

"To tell the truth, I can't make head or tail of what's going on here. These computers!"

"You want to come up?"

"Okay."

"Hop a cab and meet me at Max's."

Bert was so busy, I could just wave to him and slip out.

The day of the run-through it rained. Thunder and lightning. We all had met at the doctor's office to get our shots. Louis Jourdan was there, too.

Alan was bringing Frances Douglas to the run-through, so I went to the theater with Louis Jourdan and his wife, who was an attractive blond European lady. Everybody was a little high because of the run-through, except the doctor, who was a little low because of it. He was not invited.

So far we had seen only separate scenes of the play, with Barbara Harris holding back and holding back and as of yesterday still using her script. But today we were going to see the show strung from end to end for the first time. Not the simplest medium, the musical theater.

By now the stage managers had their scripts marked for every moment of the play. It was a map of every line, every

scene change, piece of stage business, prop, music, every movement that anybody made, showing them how to run the show
minute by minute. The only thing missing was the lighting.
The light cues would be put in in Boston.

We were not expecting a performance in depth. That would
grow in the weeks ahead. But the pacing should begin to come
through, the sound of the show, some punctuation.

One of the girl dancers had just come from a fitting and was
wearing her eighteenth-century costume. Multiply her by
twenty, and Mozart might walk in.

Alan sat in the dark with his lady in mid-theater. I slipped
into the seat beside him with my clipboard and flashlight pencil
that Bert had bought for me way back during *Camelot*.

Alan was at his happiest. He seemed to bloom when there
was a lot of hustle and bustle. If he felt any qualms about setting
in motion, with only his pencil, all this lavish expenditure of
money, energy, talent, and know-how, he gave no sign. At the
moment he was in his element. This was his medium. Far from
being intimidated by the large movements that took place onstage or screen, he felt at home when he was manipulating
them, and as I said, he liked to spend money almost better than
anything else.

"Cut 'Where are the others?' " Alan whispered to me. I
wrote.

Frances Douglas was chuckling. "He's divine," she said as
Louis finished his song. "Charming. Every word clear as crystal, too. I don't see what Burton Lane is complaining about."

"He's got nothing else to do. He's finished his score."

It looked as though we had a show. With a beautiful score.
Nothing grave had reared up to distress anyone. We were
proceeding on time. And even as we were getting into cars to
go home and pack, the stage crew was already up in Boston,
moving the sets into the theater and putting them up.

But before we left, there was unfinished business back at the house on Seventy-first Street. While we were away, Greg Kayne was going to come in and empty Alan's entire house in New York and put everything in storage.

The house had been up for sale for a year. A few weeks before we were to leave, the lawyer got an offer he couldn't refuse. What with papers to be signed and meetings in banks, Alan almost lost the sale by always being late, but with a lot of messengers delivering and phone calls and rushing around, the sale was completed, and it was agreed that when Alan left for Boston, he would never return to the house again. He would walk out tomorrow morning, and a period of his life would disappear forevermore. He was striking another set.

Alan was on a first-name basis with the storage people. Like others who did things for him for money, they were protective of him. Through the years their workmen had come in and packed up the remains of his various households as they became obsolete. I don't think he knew exactly what pieces of his life reposed in the clean, dark, expensive warehouse. He had never had time to liquidate the stuff.

This house had been his most extravagant. So had his love for Micheline: restless, complicated, laced with intrigue, planes missed, rewriting of wills, luggage lost, houses occupied in the country, in the city, on two continents, travel agents, servants hired and dismissed, loads of people involved in keeping them afloat, or adrift, as it turned out.

So the era was ending tonight. I was alone with Alan. It felt like old times.

"Shall we call Lillie?" he said.

Whenever an era began or ended, he called Lillie Messinger. She had been trying to reach him for three days. She had gotten only as far as me. After several promises from Alan, through me, she still hadn't spoken to him.

He dialed California. She picked up on the first ring. Al-

though she was outgrowing her usefulness for him profession-
ally (she rarely was invited anymore to sit in on business meetings), I knew that at the opening-night party she would sit at
his table, along with Frances Douglas and the big shots of the
show.

"Lillie? . . . We're sitting here. . . . Yes, Doris . . . and we
thought we'd say a last hello to you from the house. . . . Yes,
it's over. . . . I'm all right. . . . No, I really am. . . ."

He was cutting his cuticle with a little scissors and holding
the receiver without hands.

"The run-through went very well, I think," he said. I nodded vigorously. I felt so close to him.

"I think we've got a show. Barbara Harris is going to be
marvelous. Louis is charming. . . . Frances came to see it today. . . . She said she was going to call you. . . . Oh, and I got
a yacht. . . . We're going up to Boston tomorrow on it. . . .
No, she's just coming for the ride; then she's going to fly
back. . . ."

He was cheering up.

"I'll call you from Boston and let you know how it's going. . . . No, I will, I promise."

When he hung up, he had some unpleasant business to
attend to. Alan hated to fire people. He couldn't bear to do it
face to face. So he did it by letter. He dictated two to me.

"Dear Tina . . ."

Alan was not stingy with words. When he wrote a letter
breaking up a household or a relationship, he put his heart into
it. And it had been a nice little household, with Tina and
Simone taking care of him since his divorce. He felt saddened
by the inexorable changes of life. Giving up a staff of servants
and a house such as this might leave him fancy-free, but although I had seen Alan leave houses without regret, this one,
I felt, had held more of his feelings than others, and tonight he
was making sad sounds and faces. He felt left out in the cold.

"Dear Tina: It grieves me to have to write this letter to you
and tell you that I have had to sell the house. Yes, when I come
back from Boston, I am going to move into a hotel." He
stopped to think. I waited. "You have been a sweet and loyal
member of this household for three years. I would like nothing
better than to have you join the family again, one day when
I have another house. I shall miss you.

"Meanwhile, if I can help you in any way, please let Mr.
Kayne in the office know. He will be in charge here while the
furniture is being put in storage. Perhaps you will stay on and
help him, since you know the house better than anyone. Mr.
Kayne will have a check for you. Bless you."

I'm paraphrasing, but Alan knew how to get to someone's
heart. The fact is, he really felt it.

The one to Simone, the cook, was easier. She was a tough
old Frenchwoman. She understood plain language better and
would have no sentimentality about relocating.

With the letters in envelopes clipped to the inside of his
script and looking tenderly at Tina, perhaps for the last time,
he handed her clothes, which she carefully packed into suitcases to go to Boston, while I packed papers in cartons to go
up in the car with Tony the next day, different versions of
scenes, which I prayed would never be needed again.

From the doctor we had medication to tide us over until he
came up to Boston two days later.

The next morning at the airport Bert bribed someone to let
me take Teddy into the cabin instead of making him fly in the
cargo hold. Every time I stood before Bert and said good-bye
to him at an airport, my innermost romantic image of him was
aroused. Nothing he ever said touched me as much as the sight
of him at a time like this, standing with his feet apart, his
button-down collar open at the throat, a smile on his face and
pain in his eyes. I had to struggle against all the pull of his

gravity to walk down the carpet and into the tunnel leading
to the plane.

But today there was something else: bitterness in his eyes
and around the mouth. It almost would have been a relief if he
had punched me. In a minute he was going to say, "Have fun,"
which always was a sign of friendliness and good humor
toward my work. Today he said it ironically, with a little
venom: "Have fun."

I felt sudden rage and turned on him. "You think all this is
for the sake of fun," I cried.

"Well, isn't it?" Then, under his breath in the crowd waiting to go on the plane, he said in exasperation, "For God's sake,
Dotty, how many men do you have to have?"

He knew me. He was right: I loved three men. Three different looks, three styles, three different wits. I seemed to have
acquired a need for all of them. Big Max, with his false sav-
agery, dispensing his mythical powers; small Alan, extravagant, nervy, rich, confiding his fears and risk-taking talents to
me in jokes; and Bert, my romance, my mate, standing straight
and aloof now, as the line of passengers started to move toward
the plane.

Oddly, he wasn't planning a trip at that time. He was working on a proposal for *The Biography of a Drink of Water*, prophetic again, when water pollution was not yet a scandal. He
would be free to come up to see me, but I couldn't ask him
while Max was there, so I didn't know when that would be.

Neither of us suggested a date for him to come up to Boston.

Taking off in the plane, with Teddy luckily settled into an
empty seat beside me, I remembered we hadn't had much fun
in Boston five years ago with *Camelot*. And that was before
Max. How had we done it? I knew what could happen to a
show once you start fussing with it. If you're not careful, the
whole thing can come apart in the rewriting, never to be put

back properly together again. It is a regular Humpty Dumpty. I shuddered.

But why think about such a thing? One of Alan's great abilities was to hang on to the end. Never give up. He would do it. My spirits began to rise as the plane rose higher. We would be back in four weeks. And then my job would be over. I'd make it up to Bert. We'd find an apartment. It was time for the fun part of the show, with the actors, orchestra, lights, audiences. Time to watch a great big new Alan Jay Lerner musical get dressed up and move into the sets and come to life for the public.

When I walked off the plane an hour later into a new city, I felt as if I were on a holiday. Teddy was jaunty. I could feel the presence of the great coastline and Massachusetts beach towns that Bert and I had driven to one summer. I was going to the Ritz Carlton Hotel.

I had a view. The Boston Common was planted with September mums. The lake glistened; the sky was blue. I felt a slight foretaste of autumn when I opened the window. Such a civilized, small, pretty city. I took Teddy for a run in the park.

There was no sign of Alan or Bud. No messages. Not to be alone, I went out to seek the others. I walked through the park to the theater.

I had forgotten how small the Boston theater was. Only the stage crew was there, hammering, hauling, wiring. How did they fit the sets built for the large theater in New York into the small theater in Boston?

I caught a glimpse of Oliver Smith's haughty assistant overseeing the installation. They were assembling the psychiatrist's study, but off in the wings were parts of the rooftop set, peeking out from behind other layers. Three-dimensional jigsaw.

I was part of management. To be regarded with a bit of

caution, a bit of distance. Nobody was quite sure of my powers. I walked in Alan Lerner's shadow.

"The singers are at the Hotel Victoria, the dancers are in the lobby, and the actors are downstairs reading their lines." The stage manager was steering me carefully over dangerous boards and props backstage toward the front of the theater.

"Where's Alan?" he said.

"He'll be here anytime. He's driving up in the car," I lied, guarding the secret of the chartered yacht.

I wandered toward the sound of piano music. Herbert Ross was conducting a dancers' rehearsal.

"Where's Alan?" he said cordially.

"He should be here anytime now. He's driving up in the car with the chauffeur. When I see him, I'll tell him you have something to tell him," I said politely.

I went downstairs. Only the two stars and the director were rehearsing a scene. I stood in the shadows and feeling self-conscious, started to leave.

"Where's Alan? I need him to see something." It was Bobby Lewis, the director. Small and bald and plump, he had no charisma that I could see, and I thought of the theatrical Moss Hart.

"He's driving up in the car with Tony. He should be here anytime now." I started to leave. "I'll tell him you want to see him. I'm sorry, I didn't mean to interrupt."

As I tiptoed away, someone moved behind a pillar.

"What are you doing here?" I whispered to Tony. I pulled him away with me. "Everybody's looking for Mr. Lerner." We were going up the carpeted stairs. "He's supposed to be driving up with you. You'd better stay out of sight."

Outside on the street I was beginning to feel a dangerous depression. The sun had disappeared. People on the street looked purposeful. With Alan missing, I had no reason to be there. I hurried around the corner to the Victoria Hotel. The rehearsal was taking place in the old ballroom.

"There you are!"

It was Bud.

"Alan has been looking all over for you."

At a table listening to the big choral number sat Alan Lerner and Frances Douglas. At Bud's side was Susan Savage, her arms embracing her clipboard, getting an earful. The sound of the chorus was enormous in the room, the melodies enlarged to the tenth power by the choral arrangement. I slid happily into a seat beside Alan. He was looking his working best, with a bit of windburn on his face. The music filled the room, exciting everybody.

"It's going to be great," I whispered.

He squeezed my hand.

"It does sound good, doesn't it?" he said.

The voices were building to the climax of "On a Clear Day You Can See Forever," and then, in big Broadway musical style, by repeating a word (the word was "forever-and-ever-and-evermore"), they climbed to the heights and ended at the summit. Everybody was smiling. Even Burton Lane.

The next four days would be spent in the theater. The job was to make the play smooth, seamless, paced, the actors learning to play within the changing sets, wearing the costumes, singing and moving to the orchestra.

On the last night, during the dress rehearsal, Abe Feder came to create the lighting. One man prowling quietly and endlessly around the theater was an artist at placing the microphones in the right locations. The actors had to learn how to get onstage from the dressing rooms without breaking their necks or getting lost; they had to practice the costume changes that Alan was supposed to have left time for. And all the while, the stage manager and crew were developing the virtuosity it took to run the show from the wings.

"Can I do something for you?"

"Yes." Alan had his feet up on the seat in front of him. I was beside him.

"Love me," he said.

"That I do," I said.

"Do we have to stay here?" said Lisa on the other side of him. "Couldn't we go back to the hotel?"

"Don't you want to see them light the show?"

"I've been seeing it for hours." She ever so slightly snuggled up to him.

"You go back to the hotel, dear, and get a good night's sleep. You can take the car and send Tony back with it." But she stayed on.

From a board placed over seats made to be a desk with a light, Abe Feder, with headset on, was giving instructions to people somewhere in the upper regions of the theater. His assistant, a wiry little lady, was writing the cues.

His voice kept up a running interference with the dress rehearsal. The director, sitting near him, fidgeted and grumbled and was helpless.

In the old days, before the new union rules, he never had to put up with this. Dress rehearsal was separate, and one whole night was spent lighting the show while the actors stood still in their various poses. Not anymore. Combining it with dress rehearsal got on everybody's nerves, including the crew, who were rehearsing the set changes, as well as the actors, who were rehearsing their parts.

But occasionally something marvelous would happen.

I heard Abe droning some instructions to the unseen people, and in a moment onstage, behind the rooftop, appeared the most ravishing blue. It seemed classic, Aegean, soul-stirring.

"That's beautiful," I whispered.

More instructions.

Warmth on the faces. Glowing.

"Lovely."

". . . if it's true that everything that's ever happened always was happening, is happening now, and always will be happening, then for all we know the Egyptians are right over there building their pyramids while we are here building our skyscrapers," said Dr. Marc Bruckner, the psychiatrist, onstage.

"I had that experience from one of Max's shots," I said.

"Actually, I'm not sure I know what it means anymore," said Alan.

One of the actors had come on and was talking to the assistant director. He was obviously the union representative. The assistant director held up ten fingers from the stage. "Take ten minutes, everybody," said Bobby Lewis from his seat.

We had to be finished by midnight. More union regulations. Miraculously, at five minutes of twelve the curtain came down on the finale. The pianist disappeared. The actors went to change. Everybody was tired and wandered off.

"I'm worried about the length." Now there were four of us entering and exiting the car.

"Tomorrow at rehearsal should tell, shouldn't it?" I said, getting in. Susan and Lisa scrambled in behind me.

"No, dear," Alan said a little archly. "We have to wait for the audience. They're supposed to use up some time laughing and applauding."

Everybody was calling good-night on the street. They were staying at three different hotels. The Ritz Carlton was for the big shots. Some of the actors were staying at the Hilton down the street, and the dancers and singers at an old hotel in the other direction. Tonight almost everybody was going out to eat, even though everyone was exhausted.

"We have something better," Alan said as Tony drove off.

"What time did the doctor get in?" he asked.

"Just half an hour ago, Mr. Lerner. I helped him with his bag up to the room."

"Good. We'll feel better now," he said to me and Lisa.

We looked idly out at the cool September night on the Boston streets.

"Incidentally, I assume you have the alternate endings?"

"I have them."

Tony pulled up to the hotel.

"I'll have a look at them tonight. I have a feeling we may need them."

We got out.

The doctor had packed enough medicine for everybody. I had reserved a room for him on the same floor as ours. Alan wasn't waving a red flag, but he wasn't being overly discreet about the doctor either. For the moment it was more convenient to have him in the hotel. If people met and passed each other in the corridors, so be it. Alan was no longer in the mood to shield Burton Lane from an encounter. Burton wasn't about to quit at this stage.

In the absence of Max with the real thing, I had gotten in the habit of giving myself one of the small shots in my hip every time I felt myself getting ragged. They kept me from sleeping but didn't make me feel good. Now, as the doctor slowly pushed the lever, I felt unbelievably clarified again, as though I had been living a half-life for the two days before he came. Alan was holding a piece of cotton to his arm and looking at me in the mirror. Our eyes met. He smiled. So did the doctor. I cast my eyes down. It was too intimate.

The day of the opening night in Boston I passed in an intense daze, a kind of heightened monotony, lazing in my seat, listening to the others, watching the activities on the stage, in the theater, jumping up to find my way down the

aisle and up onstage to deliver a message, smiling and saying
hello to the actors, the stage crew, the dancers, who had
begun to realize this strangely excited, turned-on female was
no management spy.

A certain hush came over the theater as the first usher appeared. We were still two scenes away from the finale. Coffee
cartons, cigarette butts, coats, clipboards, actors and dancers
sprawling in the seats littered the theater, while the ushers in
black dresses started stacking programs. Unbelievably, it was
already seven. We had to quit.

We fled through the lobby, where men in tuxedos had gathered to take tickets. In an hour the house would be filled with
first-nighters, and the overture would begin.

Water. Water is reviving, refreshing; it softens the features.
I splashed and splashed hot, then lots of cold water on my face.
When I emerged from my hotel room, I looked better.

Alan was gone, and his room was locked. The doctor had
vanished. I needed a shot. They must be at the theater already.
I ran to the elevator, grabbed a cab.

The front of the theater was milling with people dressed for
the opening. I ran around to the stage door. It was after eight.
A few minutes to curtain time. I needed my shot. Backstage
it was chaos.

"Have you seen the doctor?"

"I saw him going into Louis's dressing room about ten
minutes ago," said Bud.

"Are you looking for that strange-looking man with the
glasses?" It was one of the dancers.

"Yes, the doctor."

"He's looking for Barbara's dressing room."

Barbara's dressing room door was ajar. Barbara was standing
nervously in front of the mirror like a patient committed to
surgery, while the hair man was adjusting her hair. Behind her,

Max, looking a little wild in his haste, was bending down sticking a needle into her hip.

"Is this all right?" Barbara said to me in the mirror in a tense voice.

"Absolutely," I said, longing to hold out my arm.

"You'll hear for yourself if it's all right when you get out there," muttered the doctor. He was packing up.

I looked imploringly at him.

"I need a little help," I said in a small voice as we left.

He had never turned on me before.

"Did you eat?" he said in a martyred tone.

"No."

He raised his hand to heaven and shrugged. "So what do you expect?"

"I'm sorry." I felt ready to faint. "We have ten minutes, if you could be so kind."

He looked at me disgustedly. "Come." He led me out to the front of the theater, where, in the back of my mind's eye, I saw people in evening clothes coming in and sitting down.

"You're going to make me late," he snarled.

He went through a door in the lobby and up some stairs across a corridor in what had become a deserted office building since nightfall. He opened a door. It was an office with a rolltop desk and an overhead bulb. He ripped open his bag, tore a syringe package, and pulled out the disposable syringe. Fumbling through the vials, he began to mix a potion. He angrily stuck the needle into my vein and, for the first time, pushed the lever all the way with one big push. I didn't care. We raced down the stairs, and suddenly, with all my heart's new ease, I found myself in the midst of opening night.

Bostonians know they're a tryout audience. They can be tough. But opening night of an Alan Jay Lerner musical any-where was a celebration.

The house was filled. The orchestra members were waiting in the pit. I could hear the bassoon and violin warming up when I showed the doctor to a seat and sat down in my own next to Alan's empty one in the last row on the aisle.

I saw Oliver Smith slouching long-legged and reassuringly casual and unworried nearby. He had designed hundreds of shows.

The lights were dimming.

"Where the devil have you been?" Alan slipped into his seat beside me.

"Right here," I said.

The conductor entered. Applause. It was an expectant audience, excited, a show-me audience. He raised his baton for the overture. Instruments up, and suddenly we were plunged into music. Brass. Woodwinds. A flood of strings sweeping over all and carrying us in the arms of Burton Lane's melodies, which were orchestrated into an opiate state of bliss. I felt myself go. I petted Alan's sleeve and smiled at him in the dark. I was in a kind of agonizing rapture of empathy for everyone. I felt for Alan, whose last three years of work were about to be laid bare for all to sample and criticize. Every word, every moment, was on trial, to be taken with delight or passed over unnoticed. No wonder he wore dark glasses.

I felt for the actors, who had to face the audience for the first time, with nothing but themselves to offer.

The curtain was rising, and there was applause for Oliver's set. A door opened, and out stepped Louis Jourdan. Irascible, impatient, irreverent, Alan's favorite kind of hero, he strode out, calling for his secretary with all the assurance of a lifetime of star performances. I slid down in my seat and relaxed.

That this big festive show was pouring out whole and effortlessly, with coherence and style, when only an hour ago it had been in pieces was a miracle to me. And although I could anticipate every word that was coming, tonight it was a new

experience, for the last missing ingredient was there: the audience, ready to give back its listening silence, its laughter and
applause.

It was going to be a hit.

By intermission I had two pages of notes from Alan. Nothing big. Notes on performance, notes to the director, to the
stage manager, notes to tighten the weave as much as possible,
so that no sign of a seam showed; notes to trim, heighten,
shape.

I wandered in the crowded lobby with Lisa, trying to pick
up people's comments. It was dense and noisy. People were
smiling and talking a lot. Boston society was there.

"They love it," we said to Alan, bursting into the manager's
office. "Did you hear the applause?"

Burton Lane was swiveling back in a chair; Bud, the general
manager, and Irving Squires, representing business, were
there. Oliver Smith, tall and smiling, was leaning against a
wall. Susan Savage was standing next to Alan.

"They love the score," I said excitedly. "They're talking
about the score—the lyrics."

"It's going to be fine," said Oliver simply.

Alan was pacing. I went to the typewriter and started to
type my notes.

"Louis and Barbara play charmingly together, don't you
think?" said Alan.

"We'll see how he sings 'On a Clear Day,' " said Burton.

We heard the bell.

"We'll see what time the curtain comes down is what we'll
see," said Alan, clenching his teeth a little.

We waited for the lights to go out before we went to our
seats. The orchestra was playing. The audience was part of the
show now, involved, affectionate even, humming the tunes as
they came back to their seats to live it out to the end.

But at ten of eleven, when there was no end in sight, they began to get a little restless.

Alan looked at his watch. We had to be out of the theater by eleven o'clock or pay overtime. Enough overtime to make profits shrivel.

A man and woman walked quickly and embarrassedly up the aisle and out.

Alan got up and paced in the back. The jokes were still working, the songs were, but the scenes were losing shape.

Cutting, I thought. It needs to be cut. With the audience there, certain lines that nobody had ever noticed in rehearsal became superfluous. Somewhere in the middle the show became heavy and began to list.

But it wasn't anything that couldn't be fixed. I heard them laughing; I watched them listening. They were loving it. Applause. The audience and the actors had become old friends. They were still willingly following Alan to the end. It just needed to be cut. It was eleven-thirty. About ten couples had walked out. Baby-sitters had to go home. By tomorrow night it would already start to be trimmed. Alan had three weeks to get it down to size.

At around eleven-forty the last chorus ended. Daisy Gamble and Marc embraced, and the curtain came down. The applause was briefer than it would have been forty minutes earlier. The theater was emptied within five minutes.

VIII

Most of the trouble was in the second act. It's the second act which tells you whether you have a show or not.

"It can be fixed," said Oliver Smith, biting into a sandwich. I never saw him lose his cool, even when the turntables in *My Fair Lady* wouldn't work.

Two carts with white linen from room service were piled with sandwiches and coffee.

But if collaboration means laboring together, that was not what was happening at this meeting after the show. Everybody was laboring on and for his own.

"I still would like to see a singer in the role" was Burton Lane's contribution. He had been huddling darkly with Bud Widney, talking about John Cullum. He was the singer whom Richard Burton had befriended in *Camelot,* who had become Burton's understudy. John Cullum was a name that some people in the theater knew.

"That's not the problem, Burton," Alan said quietly. He had been sitting with his feet up on the couch, listening thoughtfully to everybody with an inner look on his face.

Irving Squires, the general manager, said it cost thousands of dollars to pay overtime. He hoped some scenes could be cut out by tomorrow night. Bobby Lewis and Herbert Ross were there.

"Let me sit up with it and see what I can do," Alan was

saying. Everybody was exhausted. They were glad to leave him to wrestle with it.

He sat with Bud and me and Susan and Lisa, who wouldn't leave. I waited for him to produce magic, as he had in *My Fair Lady*.

At 2:00 A.M. Bud went off to bed. At 3:00 Susan was dispatched.

Alan and Lisa and I went in search of the doctor. He was in his room, sitting on the bed, sleepily giving himself a shot.

"What do you think, Max?" Alan said, flopping down on the other bed.

Max nodded his head. "It can be all right."

"It needs more than casual cutting," Alan said thoughtfully. "There's something wrong with the structure."

"Be careful," said the doctor.

"What do you think of Herb Ross's idea for a big dance number?"

"I hate it," I said impulsively.

"You're wrong, dear," he said, with a little edge in his voice. "It could work." He thought with his eyes closed. "It would eliminate three scenes."

And five characters, I thought. The whole family. I wondered how he'd fill the emptiness.

"We wouldn't need any new sets," Alan was saying. Nobody spoke. "Well, I'll think about it," said Alan suddenly, abruptly dismissing me from the conversation.

Max was ready to give him a shot.

"Hey," Alan said, suddenly brightening. "You haven't seen the yacht. Let's go see the yacht. We could even work on it for the rest of the night."

We went. We packed our scripts and clipboards. I carried the doctor's bag, and we piled into a taxi and went into the dark.

"Nobody knows about this yacht, you know," said Alan. "You two and Bud, and that's all."

I thought: He's added Bud to the secret.

The cab pulled up at a pier. There wasn't a soul around. It was chilly, but we didn't feel it. We could hear the water lapping. The big restaurant at the end of the pier was in darkness, but there were lights in the water, coming festively from the eighty-five-foot yacht. It was all white and gleamed in the dark.

The length of four ample living rooms, it was a ship worthy of a Greek tycoon. It could cross the ocean. The dining room, with high-backed chairs and a mahogany table, sat eight. It had four double staterooms, with beautiful woods, luxurious fittings, and a crew of five.

We went carefully down the long ramp that led to the ship.

"I told the captain to leave the lights on," said Alan, going up the gangplank and onto the deck. We followed. All this had cheered Alan no end.

"I can at least start cutting lines for tomorrow night's performance," said Alan, settling down in an upholstered bamboo chair.

We were wide-awake from Max's shots.

By dawn's light on the water, Alan had done some substantial cutting of lines. I marked my script and typed.

"I hate to leave here." Alan sighed, putting down his script. "It's so peaceful."

Then Max said, "I'm leaving you some medication to get you through until I come up again."

I was shocked. I didn't know he was leaving. One of Alan's secrets. When would he come back?

Alan said something strange. He said, "I'll call you, Max."

"I've arranged things so I can come every other day," said the doctor. "I wouldn't let you down."

"Why don't we wait and see?" said Alan, in a surprisingly offhand tone of voice. "And I'll call you."

What a critical time for Alan to experiment with independence from Max. He was experimenting with mine as well. I suddenly remembered one day at the doctor's office when Roscoe Lee Browne said to me, "Alan wouldn't be happy if he didn't have someone he could leave."

"If that's what you want," the doctor said, hurt. "But remember," he added a little ominously, "it takes a few hours for me to get here."

By the time we left the boat, the crew was up and dressed in whites. They had served us coffee and little muffins. Tony was called. Daylight was chill and sunny. The yacht and the harbor and the sea gulls were magnificent.

My heart sank as I got out with Teddy at the Ritz Carlton Hotel behind Alan and Lisa and watched Tony drive away with the doctor to the airport. He sat in the back of the great car, holding the precious bag and looking like some old impresario going off on a tour of Europe and leaving us behind.

The reviews weren't bad. They didn't harp on the obvious length problem. I was reading the cuts to Bobby Lewis. "Page thirty-three, line seven . . . 'In the case of such a conclusive contingency,' cut." Poor Tony, I thought. His line that was headed for immortality. Bobby Lewis would put the cuts into rehearsal at eleven o'clock this morning, and the lines would be gone that evening.

"How much do you think you've cut?" Susan said.

I winced.

"I haven't a clue," said Alan dangerously.

"Can't you estimate it?"

"Relax, Susan. We'll see tonight."

That night's performance was only five minutes shorter. The meeting in the hotel room was longer. Alan hadn't made the real incision yet.

The hotel suite was a shambles. Waiters were wheeling in carts with breakfasts, lunches, dinners, and rolling out old carts and trays. Newspapers and script papers were strewn and crumpled on the floor and furniture. The bedroom was unslept in, but in disarray from everybody lolling around on the beds and clothes abandoned all over.

Susan and Lisa had now become ubiquitous. At six in the morning Bud had gone off to sleep. I went to my room to take a bath and change.

Two days after the doctor went home, I began to feel very jittery. The medication he had left me wasn't working. Sleep, in brief snatches, was infrequent and unsatisfying. Why was Alan not calling the doctor? How long could we go on without him? When would he call? Suppose the doctor was offended and refused to come?

I lay down on the bed. I must have dozed because the telephone woke me up. It was 7:00 A.M.

"Hello?"

"Where did you go?" said Alan impatiently.

"I'm here."

"All right. Now listen carefully. Don't come back to my room." His voice was hushed, conspiratorial. "Pack a bag. Wait fifteen minutes. Then go downstairs. Don't let anybody see you, do you hear? Get into a cab and meet me at the boat. If you run into anybody, and I mean anybody, especially any little person that looks like she's looking for me, go back upstairs. Wait and try again. But hurry, hurry, dear."

Early morning in the Ritz Carlton was brass-polishing time. Newspapers in front of doors. Room service carts clattering down carpeted corridors. The waiter looked with unsurprised eyes at me slipping past him. There was always some girl or other tiptoeing down the hall. Behind Burton Lane's door there was silence. No sound came from Herb Ross's. Past Susan's door, I took a breath. I stood behind a post while I waited for the elevator. When it came, I ducked into it with a sigh of relief. No lady going to meet her illicit lover had ever navigated with more care than I did that morning as I left the hotel.

"Are you sure nobody saw you?"

"I don't think so."

"Just because I'm in the hotel, everybody thinks they have the right to call up or walk in and give me advice. And I mean every little last person." He looked at me significantly. "You and I are going to stay here until we get this show down to size."

Alan did radical surgery; he decided to cut out the psychiatrist's family. He and Bud had talked for two days about it. Painstaking work, but he hoped he would lose a big chunk of time. It meant giving up a whole comedic portion of the musical. He would try to rescue some of the gags, of course, but the family had to go. Bud was all for it. I felt Alan was being reckless, acting out of control, but I didn't say a word.

"Let's go to work," he said to me, clipping fresh yellow paper onto his clipboard.

With the doctor away, Alan was not looking good. His eyes had begun to water. He had developed a cold sore on his lip. He couldn't seem to find a way to be comfortable. The skin around his eyes was raw from wiping them almost constantly for two days.

I had terrible palpitations. I sat frozen like a stone in a bamboo chair meant for luxuriant pleasure. The skin on my face was beginning to feel as if it were stretched.

"Page eighty-seven," Alan said in a small, tight voice. "Cut from line nine, the rest of the page." He turned a page. "Page eighty-eight, cut to line . . . let me see . . . line sixteen. . . ." He wiped at his eyes.

I was horrified. He was falling apart. So was I. What was

keeping him from calling the doctor? What if we were hooked?
Was this the time to quit? I ventured: "Do you think you might
want to call Max?"

He looked up and eyed me suspiciously.

"You know," he said, "the shots may be all right for men,
but I don't think they're the best thing in the world for
women." He stared at me. "If I were you, I'd be careful."

Women? Careful? What's he up to? I thought. Are we having withdrawal symptoms? I couldn't believe it.

Another hour passed. Alan put down his script and said
wearily, "I think I'm getting a migraine headache. Call the
doctor."

Nighttime. There is fog. Visibility zero. The airfield is
empty. Tony and I are waiting in it. Standing in nowhere, I
scan the sky.

"What time is it, Tony?"

"Midnight. What do you think we ought to do?" he said
to me.

"Continue to wait, of course."

We waited. The air was chill, with the promise of a change
of season. I kept trying to get a deep breath but could draw
only a shallow one. My hands shook.

"Listen."

There was a small sound in the sky. "Do you hear it?"

"I hear a minimal sound," said Tony.

The sound got louder, then very loud, and suddenly out of
the fog, coming to rest almost at our feet, with a reassuring
noise of motors and propeller whirring, was a tiny airplane.

The door opened, and he was there, the alchemist, big, vivid,
muttering, waiting for the pilot to help him down.

"I've never been so happy to see anybody," I said, kissing
him warmly on the cheek.

"I'll bet," he said as we walked arm in arm to the car.

I was in love with the man.

Nobody may ever know what it was the doctor gave. But what we did know was that it took away Alan's headache instantly. His eyes stopped leaking at once. Within a few hours the cold sore had healed. It worked. And he worked.

I felt released into a heightened sense of normality, as one does after a bout of sickness. And more. I didn't care that Alan eyed my happy face a little resentfully.

"Look at you," Max said to me. "Go look in the mirror."

I saw a sparkling, happy image, and around me the state-room, like a room at the Pierre Hotel, worthy of an ambassador or a princess painted blue with redwood cabinets. The bathroom was fitted in tortoiseshell with gold or brass dolphin faucets. I felt at home here.

By morning Alan had just completed the last changes. The sound of my typing filled the lounge like machine-gun fire. Max was gazing out the porthole overlooking the water. There were foghorns sounding. Tony would come to rush the pages down to the Boston mimeo shop, who had to copy them fast enough to get one set to the director to study before the rest of the pages were passed out at rehearsal.

When Bud appeared in the doorway after breakfast, we were getting more shots. We weren't fooling around any longer. There was no talk of the doctor's going home. He was dressed in white sneakers, a knitted shirt with an anchor on the pocket, stretched over his ample belly, and khaki pants. He dressed like a younger man. He once had been athletic.

"Hey," said Bud heartily, fresh from a night's sleep. "How's it going?"

"Is everybody looking for me?" said Alan.

"And how."

"What did you tell them?"

"I've been trying to hide, too. Lisa has been telling them she doesn't know."

"I think I may have it licked," said Alan quietly, pursing his lips. "I've taken out the family." He delivered it resignedly.

"Great. It has to come out of somewhere."

Alan sighed. "It's too bad. They were funny."

Bud shrugged.

"I've managed to save some of the jokes. We'll put it into rehearsal today."

"The sooner the better. I suppose you want me to fire the five actors?"

"No. That's the manager's job. What I want you to do is get in touch with him so he can do it before the rehearsal starts. I don't want to come to the theater and have to see people who are fired and don't know it yet."

Bud went to the phone.

"And be sure he knows, of course, that they have to play once more tonight."

"Right."

I said to Alan, "It's amazing how the actors can do it: read the new pages today in rehearsal and still play the family version for the audience tonight."

"I work harder," said Alan.

When we arrived at the theater, Susan Savage swooped down on us.

"Where have you been for two days?"

Alan got up and went down to sit with the director.

"Where were you, Doris?"

"Working."

"Where did you go?" It was a little scream.

"Sh-h-h, listen to this. It's new."

" 'If it's true that everything that's ever happened always was happening, is happening now, and always will be happening, then for all we know. . . .' " Marc, the psychiatrist, was no longer telling it to his lively family; he was telling it to his friend Conrad.

We stayed at the theater till midday. It was painstaking and tedious. All of a sudden Alan rose and said to me, "Come on." Lisa and Susan jumped up. Three of us followed him out of the theater and into the Rolls.

I sat in front with Tony. Susan, who had been given to Bud but had taken Alan, was on one side of him, and Lisa, gentle and spaced-out in her white California coat, was buried deep in the tan leather. It was a bracing September day in the Boston neighborhood around the Ritz Carlton Hotel. The park of the Commons spread out in front, with the lake and the swan boats. Behind the hotel, small, rich, civilized streets. In the hotel Teddy waited.

We wandered into Bonwit Teller four abreast. I was very tired, but didn't have the energy to break away. I have always been slow to act on my feelings.

Susan Savage began handling shirts for Alan. So did Lisa. I had become a member of a harem on a shopping spree. Alan fiddled restlessly with the merchandise.

As much as Alan didn't want to be alone, he seemed to be embarrassed by this scene, shopping with three females at the shirt counter at Bonwit's.

Suddenly, to my own surprise, I simply turned and strolled to the front of the store, where I could see the sunshine.

Alan broke away and came after me. "Where are you going?" He stood there, his eyebrows straining upward, his mouth in a grimace of discomfort, looking almost comical in his predicament. "I want to be with *you.*"

I almost melted, so habituated had I become to his company. But instead, I said, "And I want to be with Teddy. I'm going to take him for a run in the park. He's been cooped up alone in the hotel room for hours."

*   *   *

That night we went to see the family's last performance.
There they were, just as lively, quarrelsome, and funny as ever,
though all day long they'd sat in the theater watching themselves being wiped out of existence. Their bags were packed
in the hotel, yet they played with all the enthusiasm of people
in a snapshot at a party long gone by.

But the following night, despite their departure and all the
cutting and manipulating, the curtain came down only ten
minutes sooner. And with the family gone, the play lost color;
there were some awkward transitions. Some of the texture had
been loosened, leaving exposed longer speeches about life and
time, without the lighter moments that came from the family.
Marc was directing his dialogue only to his friend Conrad. The
stage seemed too empty.

There was another noisy meeting in the hotel room, in
which nothing was solved, after which we all went to the boat.
Max, too.

The boat was no longer a trysting place or a secret. Alan had
made a date to go on a little overnight cruise with Frances
Douglas, but he was in too deep even for him to play hooky,
and he didn't want her to see the show the way it was. He
postponed the cruise.

So this magnificent white oceanwise yacht with a crew of
five in white ducks turned into a kind of local ferry, cruising
under full power between the pier, where it came to pick us
up, out to the marina, a twenty-minute ride, where it berthed
at night, a star among the lesser boats. When we were ready
to return to the theater, the crew would start up the motors,
and the yacht would steam back to the pier, where Tony
would meet us in the Rolls-Royce. This was the only way Alan
could enjoy his yacht. Sometimes the signals would get crossed
and Tony arrived to pick us up at the pier, only to find the

watery space empty. Then he would race to the marina or the theater looking for us.

Teddy needed a haircut. His slim face and form were sinking into shapeless, curly brown fur, except for his eyes, grown mournful with tedium and a terror at the sound of the boat's motors. I would have to hold his shaking body tight during the run between the pier and the marina. Alan became openly hostile to my first child, said that he was the only Jewish poodle he'd ever met and that my attachment to Teddy was a bit strange. His telling me he was jealous of Teddy didn't calm my growing feeling that if not actually among strangers, I was with people who were keeping me from taking care of my own: Teddy and Bert. I had allowed the days to slip by without calling Bert.

Bud came and went. Susan slept. Kitty Hart came one night to see the show and stayed over on the boat. We talked about her husband, Moss, long gone now, and how much Alan wished he were here. Lisa was slowly fading, all except her wide eyes. She and Alan and I and the doctor stayed up every night.

I had given up sleeping altogether. Once in a while I would lie down in my stateroom. It seemed to me I weighed a thousand pounds and could feel myself sinking into a bottomless depth, my mind clear and bright and aimless, my body deadweight, except for my fingers, which noticed my hipbones had grown prominent by loss of weight.

"Did you eat?"

"No. Can't."

"You have to. Here." The doctor handed me a roll from the tray. I munched on it.

"I didn't sleep." A deliberate come-on. His bag was open on the couch. The ship's lounge was a mess from too much of the wrong kind of use.

"You don't need to sleep. You think you do, but you don't. Here." He probed my inner arm for a vein, found it. After the glorious pause he said, "Well?"

"I feel as if I slept eight hours!" I threw my arms around him and kissed him on his warm neck. "Thank you," I said to this big, commanding, life-giving man, whose presence had become essential to me. It seemed to me that fate, not I, was leading me to him. I was in too deep to retreat.

Besides, Bert hadn't come up to see me. He didn't need me, and he wouldn't let me need him. I saw our marriage as a kind of amateur attempt. Despite the chicken paprika, I wasn't a wife, and he, backing off and letting me slip away, wasn't a husband. My heart dropped as I felt us splitting apart. Bert was self-sufficient. He went about his business alone.

He was probably getting a divorce right now.

"What do you want?" Max said after I had kissed him.

You, I thought. But I said, "I want to talk about Alan's birthday party."

"You're giving him a party?"

"Just a little champagne and cake with the company."

"When is his birthday?"

"A week from Friday."

"He's going to be forty-five, you know," he said warningly.

"We don't have to say that. The whole company will be there. He might be hurt if we ignored it. Bud is going to get Bobby Lewis to call a meeting onstage that night after the performance, and it will just turn into a big surprise."

I had toyed with the idea of calling Mrs. Douglas and inviting her to come up, but when I looked around at the mess and at the doctor needing a shave, with his head nodding and a little puffing of his lips every time the breath came out, the idea subsided.

"What's a surprise?"

Alan entered in bare feet, yawning, hair freshly brushed and damp, and I caught a whiff of my favorite after-shave lotion.

"You are," I said, smiling. "You surprised us."

The look of resentment which I thought I saw in his eyes was gone, and he flopped down on the couch beside me and took my hand.

"Let's work."

"What are you going to do?"

"The ending. Nobody likes it. I'm going to read the other two to the cast tomorrow and put it to a vote. I'm tired of thinking about it. Let *them* decide."

"You're going to let the cast decide which ending to use?" I was being judgmental.

"Why not? Do you think it's sacred?"

"I dunno." I had assumed that after a whole evening of show there could be only one way that it could all come inevitably to rest.

"You're right," he said, "you don't know."

The next day he put it to a vote, as he said he would. The cast wanted Marc and Daisy to go off in a blaze of light in the airplane, no matter what the rational arguments against it were.

The director and the choreographer worked out a big walk toward the plane; it was decided the choral arranger should be called in New York to enlarge the music and put the changes on a plane that night; Abe Feder in New York redid the lighting by phone, and the whole cast was repositioned in the airport. We spent the afternoon in rehearsal. It wouldn't shorten the play, but it made everybody happier.

As Alan settled in for the siege, the yacht became a battleship. He almost never got up from his chair anymore. He had a grim look in his eyes, and when he moved, it was almost slow motion. He could concentrate only briefly and lapsed into little dozes.

Burton Lane never came to the boat, but the word from Bud was that Burton wanted Louis Jourdan out of the show and John Cullum in. If the play was going to go down, he wanted at least to rescue his score. Bud was beginning to go in Burton's direction.

I was aghast. They wanted to remove a big star and put in a singing actor. To be honest, I thought, Louis's character, Marc, was not the most developed. But he did have charm. That was what Alan could write when all else failed. Louis Jourdan's charm was persuasive.

"We've taken the liberty of speaking to John Cullum. He could go in on two days' notice," said Bud, puffing on his pipe and looking deceptively casual.

"I wish you hadn't," said Alan.

"It wasn't my decision."

"I hope Louis doesn't suspect any of this."

"If he does, he hasn't indicated it."

"Burton wants to put John in the role."

Alan looked at me as he said it, and I knew he didn't want this.

"We'd have to pay off Louis. It would cost a fortune," Alan said.

"Burton thinks it's worth it. And who knows? Maybe with a big lyrical voice like John's, the show would pick up some. It won't solve the job of cutting; you still have to do that. But this might help."

Alan said, "I wonder how Louis would take it?"

"Louis is a gentleman. I think he'd be the first one to understand. You know, he himself had doubts about singing the part."

"But I overcame them for him," said Alan. "I taught him how to deliver the songs."

He looked at me and the doctor, back at Bud. I kept my mouth shut. Alan looked down at his hands, and there was silence while he thought. When he spoke, it was with resignation.

"I guess I'm the one who has to speak to Louis. Call him in his room," he said to me, "and see if I can come and have breakfast with him."

But Louis Jourdan didn't want to give up his part. He'd put a lot into it. He wanted more time to try harder. He asked for another week.

As Alan told this to Bud in the hotel room after breakfast with Louis, he looked at me with concealed excitement. There was no doubt in my mind that he was delighted with Louis's position and that he would rescue him.

"I guess we have to give the guy his chance," said Alan to Bud. "We can't just sweep him out like dust."

Bud nodded noncommittally.

"Well," said Alan, getting up and squinting at himself in the mirror, "I told Bobby Lewis I'd stop by his room and have a chat. I'll meet you all at the theater."

My attention lapsed (detachment that came with the shot). The next time I noticed, everybody had left, and I was lying on the couch alone in the room with Bud. Whether he saw me or not, he lifted the phone and called New York. It was Louis Jourdan's agent.

"Alan wants Louis out" is what I heard. "Speak to him— will you?—and explain it's not as if he'll lose anything. He can go off on vacation on full salary, for the good Lord's sake."

I was very confused. I was positive Alan had just told me with his eyes he didn't want to switch leading men. But I knew Bud would never do this on his own. Alan must have said the opposite to Bud. I took it as another sign of Alan's giving in to pressure.

On Thursday night John Cullum went in and played Marc. Where Louis Jourdan was light, John Cullum was lightweight.

Alan had given up control. Louis Jourdan as Marc was

already a memory. He never played the part again. He and his wife left the next day, and with them a certain classiness went out of the show. I felt it was a turning point in the disintegration of a musical, and I was beginning to resent Alan's surrender.

He was developing a bitter look around the mouth. He was constantly meeting with Bud, who was developing a crinkly, anxious look around the eyes. All you could see of his mouth through the beard were two full lips.

Removing a big chunk that could come out had led nowhere. It looked as if the cuts were going to come from here, there, and everywhere. Susan was running back and forth with Tony to the copying people, delivering pages every day to the director, who would pass them out and put the new material into rehearsal.

Alan didn't go to rehearsals anymore. He was too busy writing. We went to the performances at night.

Performances were one step behind rehearsals, and because there was always enough new material to keep the actors slightly on edge and holding back in the new parts, the performances were uneven, sometimes shaky, tentative. They played what was left of the old play bigger, and the audience seemed confused.

The actors brought their usual good-natured gallantry to the learning of the new lines, but people were being stretched to the limit. The grimness around Alan's mouth stayed.

"Cut 'If it's true that everything that ever happened always was happening' et cetera."

I gasped.

"What's the matter, dear?" he said testily.

"There goes my favorite speech."

He shrugged. "You're acting like an investor. Bud says they don't understand it."

I looked at the doctor. He was turning the pages of a magazine. Alan was relying more and more on Bud.

"Don't interfere," Max had said to me. "You'll end up holding the bag."

But I did. One day Alan was working on a scene to adjust the irrational new ending, where Marc and Daisy, for no apparent reason, are in love.

Daisy, waiting for Marc in his office, accidentally switches on a tape that spills the beans. The mystery girl whom everybody's talking about, and who under Marc's hypnosis reincarnates to eighteenth-century Melinda, is she.

Daisy runs out, feeling used. She's been a mere vessel for Melinda to live in. When Marc comes in and finds her gone, he sings the urgent "Come Back to Me," saying he'll hound her, track her down wherever she is. For it is she who carries within her the girl he's fallen for, and he won't let Daisy deprive him of her. It never seems to occur to him that she may be the same girl.

When he finally finds Daisy on her rooftop, he's desperate to get her back in her chair. Like Henry Higgins with Eliza Doolittle, he treats her without respect.

Daisy is angry: "You want me back to see *her*. . . . I'm not anything like Melinda. . . . All I know is what I'm like, and I don't like it. Nothing can change me. I have no character. I don't know if there is a person called Melinda, but I know she's not me. . . ."

I ventured to say to Alan, "Mightn't he get angry at Daisy for refusing to become Melinda? Rave at her? Take her by the shoulders and try to shake Melinda out of her? Because down deep, don't you think he suspects that somewhere inside Daisy's shrinking violet is the princess he loves, that Daisy and Melinda are one?"

Alan didn't take to it. "Listen," he said. "Everybody has an idea what they want this show to be. Now don't *you* start. At this point all I want is to get through this decently." His mouth slackened, and he added plaintively, "If I ever get out of this alive."

I had the feeling he couldn't write in his condition.

The day of the birthday party it started to rain while we were on the water, steaming into the harbor.

The cake, which I had gone into town to order on a pretext, was going to be delivered that evening to the dancers' dressing room. The champagne would be on ice. Bud had arranged that the company would pay for it, and the lights would be kept on in the theater after the performance.

Alan was looking depressed today, with his script forever open on his lap.

"What a way to spend one's life," he said, looking up and stretching his arms. "Words, words, words. You could wake up one day and find while you were doing all this, you turned into Rip Van Winkle."

I smiled. "You didn't."

If Alan knew I knew he had turned forty-five, he didn't say so. I was afraid to give away the surprise party, so I didn't wish him happy birthday. Nobody else did either. It was turning into a somber day.

That night, after the performance, after the meeting on-stage, the whole company was going to burst into "Happy Birthday to You" at a sign from the director. Burton Lane would be at the piano. Then they'd bring on the cake and open the champagne, and he'd have his birthday.

The curtain came down at eleven-ten. Every night Alan managed to lop off a few precious minutes. But the play had become emptier, and every cut took a little of the juice out of it. I had lost my ability to see the show, and I sat in a kind of stupor of exhaustion and boredom. It was beginning to look like a silhouette of a show.

The audience started to leave, and Alan got up.

"Let's go."

We slipped down the aisle and up onto the stage. Bud was coming from the other side. We met in the middle and stood around, waiting for the cast to get out of costume and into their clothes. The crew was wrapping up. The curtain rose. Alan was talking with Bud in a corner. He didn't notice the stagehands wheel in the rehearsal piano.

Barbara Harris came onstage in jeans. Alan went to her. John Cullum arrived. He was always cheerful. Why shouldn't he be? Others straggled on. Herb Ross and Burton Lane were at the piano. Standing onstage, surveying the scene, with my wan Mona Lisa smile, I suddenly got a horrible insight.

They all want to be someplace else, I thought. They're fed up. Alan is putting them through hell. Everybody's exhausted. They don't want to give a party for him. All they want is for him to finish fussing with the show and go off and leave them alone to play it. The smile on my face was fading, and I must have had a startled look in my eyes. I was having traitorous thoughts.

"It's not as if he's inventing a cure for cancer," I'd heard Bert say months ago. "All he's doing, for God's sake, is writing a fucking musical."

"Happy birthday to you. . . ."

Barbara Harris began it; everybody joined in. It was a big sound, with sopranos and tenors and basses from the chorus singing.

Alan reeled around in his place and almost cringed. A terrible look flashed across his face. I winced.

He hates it. I knew it at once.

He was smiling now, modestly, looking overwhelmed with pleasure.

The cake came on, the plastic glasses with stems, and the champagne. The stage managers poured. Everybody stood around holding a glass. There was no place to sit. There was nothing much to do. The dancers and singers were making their own party at the side of the stage. Some of them had never even spoken to Alan. The actors were making nice hearty remarks and telling stories. Alan was talking to Bud, Susan and Lisa at his side.

As I came up to wish him happy birthday, I overheard him say to Bud, "Who did this?"

"Here she is now."

Alan, turning, saw me. "Ah, little mother," he said, "it was adorable of you to do it, but how did you ever know it was my birthday?"

I was over my head. I swam anyway. "I've always known when it's your birthday."

"You have?" He looked at me as though I had spoken Chinese.

Alan and I were alone in the blue and white upholstered salon of the yacht, berthed in fog at the marina, the farthest point we could get from the theater. The crew was sleeping. Bud was in his stateroom.

We could have been back at the beginning, with fresh everything; only it wasn't the beginning. On opening night there was a play. Now there was a gutted script in our laps. A hundred professionals were scattered and tucked into rooms all around Boston, sleeping and having nightmares about the new changes the morning would bring.

Alan, taking a sip of cold coffee, said in his nonchalant way, "There's this man in Princeton named Velikovsky. . . ."

I nodded. "What about him?"

"He has a very interesting theory."

I already didn't like the sound of it. I remembered the ESP conversations we had that sounded like my mother's Christian Science testimonials.

"Is he from Princeton University or does he just live in Princeton?"

Alan went on. "He says that long, long ago everybody was very tall. There was no such thing as men and women and sex. And everyone lived peacefully and happily together. . . ."

I got up and began to pace in a small area. Images of hardship filled my thoughts. Three years of life-threatening exhaustion, three years of dragging groceries back to those dreary rooms at the Hotel 14, Bert elaborately not noticing and pretending with me that we were having dinner, even lighting candles. And he let me. And Alan let me. And for what? For some silly so-called philosophical nonsense.

Alan was saying, "Then one day the earth got too close to the moon's gravitational pull, and it tipped. And everybody got all scrambled up together and created tall and short, and men and women. And that was the beginning of sex, and ever since then the world has been filled with troubles." He looked at me expectantly.

I had always gone along with Alan. But at this moment the long disintegration of the play, Alan's surrendering control of it had sapped my energy, and it seemed like my own loss. This piddle about some man's shallow ruminations on the human condition drove me to utter recklessness. Before I could stop myself, I took the irreversible step that would shatter the unspoken vow of loyalty between us that had worked so perfectly for fourteen years.

Dramatically I said, "Doesn't that *bore* you?" I was exacting the price for his loss of genius.

He recoiled visibly. "No, it doesn't bore me."

I plopped myself into a chair, with my hand waving and cutting the air.

"What kind of scholarship is that? Anybody can invent any story in the world! Who cares about the earth tipping and people scrambling, and tall and short, and becoming male and female, and sex? Doesn't it bore you? Doesn't it bore you?"

All this was meted out quietly as we sat together in the salon of the yacht, but our long life together was crumbling as surely as if the earth had quaked. Alan was looking down at his small, square hands spread out, palms down, on the opened script. I never heard Alan raise his voice in anger, but he was angry now. And stung.

"Maybe you should work alone," I went on, wounding. "You don't need all these people around. You could work alone. Everybody is messing around in your play."

"It's not a play yet," he said, still not looking at me.

"It *was* a play. They loved it on opening night."

"Dear girl," he said now, looking at me with his feudal dismissing toss of the head, "it would seem to me you're out of your depth."

"I wish you didn't think you were."

"And it would also seem to me the best thing people can do in this life is not hurt other people." He got up and walked out of the room.

"It's all over between Alan and me," I was blurting out to the doctor, who was stepping heavily down from the little plane. He had flown to New York that morning and had arrived back in time to miss the party. Strangers helped him down, turned around, and went up the steps again. The motors were roaring. We walked toward the car.

"How was the party?"

"He hated it. He'll never forgive me for it."

"Poor girl."

"And I turned on him. I broke our bond."

He sighed. "I tried to warn you, but you wouldn't listen."

We were getting into the car. As we settled into the tan

leather seats and Tony drove off, he said to me fatally, "Maybe it's time for you and Alan to get a divorce."

"You mean, leave?"

He nodded. "Maybe leave," he said morosely.

"Before the opening?"

"Yes, now," he said in the dark of the car.

I hadn't spoken to Bert for weeks. I wouldn't call him from the yacht. And as I said, he was probably divorcing me right now.

Max was saying, "Listen, why don't you go home and marry your husband?"

"It's too late," I said.

So far the worst in life had never happened to me. No matter how bad things got, somehow they had always cleared up. When I had to have a biopsy on my breast and was in a hospital room with three terminal cancer patients, I walked away into the sunlight two days later and went back to sit with Alan on his rooftop garden. Bert was away. When I was twenty, I was attacked in my car one night and almost strangled. I rode away and forgot about it the next morning.

But now I felt the cracking of change, a shift in my landscape, and Alan was going to be absent from it, and Max belonged to Alan, and I belonged to no one.

Max was saying, "I think you and your husband could still make it."

"I've got to make a phone call," I said, bounding out of the car.

"Don't you want your shot?"

"Can I have it after?"

Max said, "Never say 'after.' "

In the hotel room I took Teddy in my arms and we looked in the mirror. Always, in the mirror, behind the surface image, I saw another: a reassuring image of the woman Bert loved.

Today I just saw a distressed, frightened female.

Bert was in his office. His hello had a freshness, a ring to it, a man engaged in action, busy, happy. I melted.

"Bert?"

"Oh, hello." Now it was his terse voice, with silence surrounding it.

"I want to come home."

Intensified silence.

"Bert?" No answer. "I want to come home." You'd think I was a gift.

"Do as you like."

"Don't you want me to come home?"

"Do what you want." He wasn't even angry.

"Don't you care?"

"No."

I didn't have the strength. I felt I could break.

Alan was speaking softly to me through my migraine headache. "I'm sorry if I hurt you, darling. I wouldn't ever want to hurt you." He was stroking my forehead.

The estrangement seemed a faraway nightmare that had passed off, leaving only the pain in my head to testify to its existence. I was lying on the sofa, in the fold again, as Max prepared shots. I closed my eyes. He would take my pain away.

"They want to postpone the New York opening," Alan said.

Silence from the doctor.

"They want to spend two more weeks here in Boston, getting it in shape for New York."

"What do you want?" Max said.

"I want to escape humiliation."

"Can you fix it in two weeks?"

"I'll have to." His teeth were clenched. "But how am I going to tell Frances about the delay?"

"Maybe call Lillie?" I said from closed eyes.

"Yeah! Thank you, dear."

After his shot he called Lillie.

"Come to New York. Talk to her, Lillie. It'd be better coming from you. She's going to want to come up. Explain why it's better if she waits there. Have lunch. Go to Centre Island. I'll get a staff. Hold her hand. I'm afraid she's going to be unhappy about this delay. I'll get a reservation at the St. Regis for you for tomorrow night. Doris will send a limousine for you to the airport. . . . The show? I don't have a clue. . . . I'm okay, I guess. . . . Call me, Lillie. . . . Good-b-y-e."

The next morning he called Frances Douglas from Boston. "Darling," he said, "Lillie Messinger is coming to New York. . . . I want you to have lunch with her. Talk to her. You can, you know. Listen to what she has to say, will you? She'll call you tonight from the St. Regis. Everything's fine . . . really . . . only five more minutes to cut. Don't worry. . . . You're not worried? Why not? . . . You don't? To tell the truth, I don't give a damn either. Call me when you see Lillie. . . . Good-bye, darling." His voice trailed off into the phone.

When Alan called Lillie in, it was a step away from intimacy. His love affair had run its course, I thought.

With the postponement I had an excuse to call Bert again, but when I got his office, they told me he was in Missouri. It occurred to me he was being excessively cruel, not telling me he was going away.

We settled into the last two weeks in Boston, but despite the reconciliation with Alan, things were not the same between us. Once planted, the seed grew. The thought that all this was not in search of a cure for the dread disease, or even the common cold, or to give homes to stray dogs, or plant trees on streets, or help people stop smoking, but merely to rescue a Broadway musical of growingly suspicious value, lingered and settled in my mind. I understood about the coming break with Alan, and

I was expecting to receive papers from a lawyer from Bert at any time, but I couldn't make a move. For the present I was just going to hand Alan his scalpel when he asked for it.

But he was cutting with a machete.

He's mad, I thought. He's mad at somebody. Burton Lane. Herb Ross. Me. Himself mostly. He's mad at everybody. He's sabotaging the show!

"Read for Bud now, will you, dear?" Alan spoke barely audibly. He was sprawled on the couch. We were on the sparkling deck of the yacht.

I read. Bud interrupted.

"That line about his lecture?"

"Well?"

"You cut out the lecture speech, remember?"

"I did?"

I had a list. "Lecture: Act One, Scene Four." I turned the pages of my script. "The lecture speech is out."

"Okay, read the line," Alan said wearily. "I'll fix it."

I read. It was a sticky cut to make. He couldn't just remove the line; it left a gap. He had to fool with it to make it come out right.

"Okay, make a note of it."

I read on.

"Where's the reminiscing dialogue?" said Bud.

"Gone."

"You need it."

"But this morning you told me to take it out!"

Bud leaned forward and said quietly, looking into Alan's face. "Well, I've changed my mind. It has to go back."

I thought: It's a case of the blind leading the blind. We're all acting crazy here.

One lovely autumn day we heard footsteps coming up the gangplank. It was shocking to think someone might violate our costly space, but the footsteps were definitely approaching.

"Anybody here?"

A splendid-looking brown-haired girl stood in the doorway.
She was smiling. She was slim and smooth and had about her
the unmistakable mark of a liberated woman, an easy, aggres-
sive confidence, crisp. She obviously felt at home in these
surroundings.

"I've been trying to get in touch with you for ages," she said
cheerfully, almost chidingly.

Fortunately all the syringes and cotton and wrappers and
paraphernalia had just been tucked away, and the lounge of the
ship was fairly decent, considering what was going on there.

"According to your office, you're unreachable, so I just flew
up here. I hope you don't mind." She must have gotten someone at the theater to tell her where he was.

Alan was summoning up charm from a hidden source.

"Why did you want to reach me?" He had actually produced a playful twinkle in his eyes and an amused, indulgent
look around his mouth.

"I want to interview you."

Her name was Karen Gundersson. She was a journalist, and
she wanted to do a free-lance piece on Alan Jay Lerner and the
great Broadway spectacle.

"If you say yes, I've got my tape recorder right here," she
said, taking the strap off her shoulder and putting the recorder
down on the table.

He was going to do it! No lawyers, no agents. He was going
to talk for her tape recorder. She was going to come to the
show that night. She was going to spend time with him, get
to know him, observe him.

"Can you believe it?" I was talking to the doctor. We were
sitting in the back of the theater. The actors had stopped taking
shots from Max.

Karen was sitting up front next to Alan. It was a rehearsal

to try out a revised scene. Alan inclined his head toward her
to listen to what she was saying. He laughed out loud.

"Relief," said the doctor.

"Comic relief," I said.

"There's nothing comic about it," said the doctor.

"There's no need for you to come back to the boat tonight,"
Alan said to me. "I'm going to knock off work."

We were in the manager's office. Max was giving him a shot,
smiling mysteriously. I had heard that he could do things for
a man's sexual powers. I stared as Alan seemed to come back
to ruddy life again.

"You'll be okay tonight," Max said, and slapped him on
the arm.

Max and I were walking down the hotel corridor, past my
room to his.

"Come, I'll give you something special."

Give me what? I thought.

He unlocked his door with the hotel key. There was no
sitting room, just a big bed. I looked longingly at it. He locked
the door.

"Lie down."

He opened his bag. He had an odd look around the shoulders, a sort of get set look.

"We have to put some weight on you before you go home,"
he said to me tenderly, leaning over me with the syringe.
"You'll be bad for my reputation."

He watched me imbibe the liquid and kept his hand on my
arm. I looked at his large, weighty, vivid, older male face
almost touching mine, as my body relaxed. He lay down beside
me with all his bulk and cradled my head in his arms. I lay
couched in the length of his body, while he crooned little love
sounds to me in German. It was the first time we were alone
together. I slid my clothes off; he, his, which he left in a heap.

He had a big belly, but a still-powerful chest and shapely legs. I almost fainted with reality. I had a sexual hunger so ravenous that I felt like a wild wolf.

He made love like a healer. He filled me. Inside, I felt as if a giant breaker were gathering out in the ocean, rising from the sea, higher, heavier, faster, getting ready for the tumbling crash—I thought, I can't live another moment of this—and then the wave didn't make it; it became a heart-catching swell that slowly spread and dissipated into the deep, its turbulence evaporating.

Maybe I was being protected from a climax that could only end in death. I went limp. He fell off me and to my side. We didn't speak. To my surprise I fell asleep to the sound of his breathing.

The telephone woke me early the next morning. I lay miserably watching Max talk into it from the bed.

"I'll come," he said into the phone. Looking at me: "No, I don't know where she is. If she comes, I'll bring her." So there was to be no time for love again.

"Next time?" I said.

He shook his head.

"Never say 'next time.' "

He was already up. "Go now and shower quickly. Alan is alone."

Alan was lounging on the bamboo couch, talking on the telephone. He beckoned to us to sit down. I thought in those tan slacks and sandals he looked as if he were on a holiday. I wondered if the splendid-looking girl he was talking to at the other end of the phone from the airport knew at what complicated, messy moment in his life she had met him. I seemed to be the only one who was aware of that. There was no visible sign of the wreck he was beneath his air of fun and audacity on the telephone.

The next time I was alone with Alan, he said, "Now you're Mrs. Doctor." I said nothing.

The rest of the stay in Boston slipped by for me in a dim, punishing miasma of monotony. Max came and went, and there was no next time.

I remember one night at the theater during a particularly tedious part of the performance, when I slipped out into the empty lobby to sit on a bench. Oliver Smith strolled up. I admired him; he was a cool, always good-natured professional. He had designed all of Alan's shows that I had worked on.

He smiled and sat next to me, with his long legs out in front of him.

"One day, Doris," he said, "we'll have lunch and talk about what happened to this show."

So it wasn't just my imagination. "It's been destroyed," I said. He nodded. We didn't talk about it anymore or ever. It was enough said.

Whatever it was Alan had done, when time ran out and the last night in Boston finally arrived, the curtain came down within a minute of the deadline, and the musicians rose from their seats and were out of the pit on the stroke of eleven. But let someone sneeze onstage, or the conductor relax one number a trifle, or a scene be just a hair's breadth slower in the playing, and we'd be into overtime. Forevermore there would be just that bit of extra stress that Alan had left for them.

Alan was going to sail home on the boat the next morning, and Karen had come up to sail back with him. They were going directly to the house on Centre Island, nobody, not anybody to know about it. To continue the interview.

The last night, on the yacht, Alan said, "Listen, I want to talk to you about something." That kind of remark has always made me feel dread. "I've told you before, if I were you, I'd cool it with the shots. I don't think they're the best thing for you."

"Why not?"

"Just accept what I say."

"You mean I don't look so hot?"

"Well, since you mention it, you *are* looking a little storm-tossed. Listen," he went on, "you don't have to worry. It's not cocaine or any of that stuff. I went for a week without a shot when I was in California, and I felt fine."

I felt reassured he was right. The doctor was too complex and interesting a man to be simply pushing drugs on us. He took the medication himself. And hadn't he cured Alan of his migraines? Alan hadn't had one since he'd started to see Max. If Eddie Fisher was afraid we were hooked, it may have been because he seemed the kind of fellow who craved to be under someone's power. He could probably become addicted to aspirin. So could I, I realized.

To my relief, Tony's footsteps coming down the deck brought an end to the conversation. I could have driven to New York with Tony the next morning, but I couldn't face five hours of conversation with him. Ever since Alan had read to Tony from the play, he was acting like a collaborator. All he wanted to do was talk about the show.

The next morning Teddy and I took the train.

IX

New York City. Two o'clock in the afternoon. Teddy and I alone. No sense in the dim hotel rooms of the brisk October weather that excites everybody on the streets.

As I opened the door, Teddy made a flying leap for his favorite green chair and curled up touchingly into it. At least *he* was home.

Bert had left a coffee cup and saucer on the table. It must have been there by itself for two weeks, ever since he went to Missouri. I paid a visit to his clothes in the closet and sank my face into his familiar tweed jacket, but it didn't help; there was no smell of him lingering in the clothing to relieve my panic.

My two suitcases lay closed in the middle of the floor.

Sitting at the edge of a tan vinyl chair, I looked around at the old living room. Not even a drawing of Howard's on the wall. Not a photograph, a vase, or the black lacquered upright piano that Bert had bought for me. Everything on hold in storage, awaiting the arrival of this monster play that had drawn me into Alan's failing universe.

I felt a sudden hatred for Bert. His righteous silence, his trips, his anger, his absence now. As I had lain next to him in the night on life's edge, gasping for deep breaths, he had slept beside me, oblivious. I hated his deep sleeping. Living under the same roof, we had managed to abandon each other with hardly a word.

It was too late to repair; I needed to see Max. The specter of a future without him and his shots drove me to the phone.

I dialed. A stranger's voice answered, not Beatrice's crooning German alto. Oddly tough. I had to give my name. I waited. The woman didn't come back. I hung up impulsively and dialed again. A "busy" signal. I had gotten into a trap. The "busy" signal would be my first call on hold. I must have dialed five more times in a row before the line was clear. At last the tough voice answered.

"I think we got disconnected," I said tensely.

"You can come."

I was told to wait in a treatment room, and who came in? Not Max, but Anna, the tragic blond Czechoslovakian beauty, who was to Max what I had been to Alan; only she was never going to turn on Max.

She prepared my shot with graceful gestures; she had lovely hands.

It became apparent I wasn't going to see the doctor. She approached my outstretched eager arm and wrapped a tourniquet around it. Slipping the needle neatly into my blue vein, she said gently, "It is time for your life to change."

As she slowly injected me, the beloved heat glowed in my throat on its healing journey through my body, but this time it was carrying with it a whisper of a treacherous truth, that something had been decided about me that she knew and I didn't. Some great rupture was going to shatter the delicate, unbearable balance my life had become.

"You will have a new life," she said in a soft, relentless tone. "You will make new friends, and after a while you will be well and happy again."

I was too frightened to move. What new life? I didn't say a word, for fear of an answer. I pulled down my sleeve and murmured, "Thank you, Anna."

*   *   *

Lillie stood by the open door, small, colorful, welcoming, as I rushed down the hall toward her. Her face fell.

"Oh, my dear," she said, "come in."

It was the St. Regis. Opulent in red and black, with crystal lamps and carved high moldings. Alan was paying for it.

I took a seat at the edge of the couch.

"It's all over between Alan and me," I said, to my utter surprise. That's not what I thought was first on my mind. But it felt like the safest disaster of my life at the moment.

"I wouldn't go so far as to say that," Lillie said kindly. So it wasn't just my imagination. She had obviously been talking to Alan.

"I turned on him, and he'll never forgive me for it," I said. "What did Alan say to you, Lillie?"

"Well," she said regretfully, "you know how Alan needs loyalty more than other people do."

"Loyal! He's trading everybody in who's over thirty. Not you, Lillie dear, never you," I added quickly. "You're the one person he'll never abandon."

"Oh, I wonder," said Lillie wistfully.

"He's mad at everybody," I said bitterly. "Why doesn't he get mad at himself for once? He wrecked the show. He let everybody mess around with it, and now he's mad at them. What's left is a bare skeleton. Ask Oliver Smith."

"I'm not interested in Oliver Smith right now; I'm interested in you."

"Me!" I said with despair. "What else did he say?"

Lillie hesitated. "Perhaps you might have been a little tactless. You know how Alan doesn't like the people he's close to to be close to each other."

"Oh, I see," I said, "with the doctor."

"Well, yes," Lillie said, again with regrets.

My voice rose with injustice. "I kept Alan company with the doctor. Nobody else would go there with him. Can you imagine Alan sitting up night after night alone? He paid for my shots because he can't stand to be alone, and now I suppose he won't pay anymore."

Lillie looked at me, as though searching.

"I took the liberty of calling Dr. Jacobsen about you," she said.

I listened acutely.

"He said you're going to be all right and happy again in a little while."

First Anna, now Lillie.

"Dotty," Lillie said, like one of the characters on 3:00 P.M. television, "are you in love with the doctor?"

It shocked me like a sock in the stomach.

She pursued it. "Would you want to marry the doctor?"

I shivered at the image of change. In Lillie's and Alan's world people tore up their lives and started new ones. What did they do with their old lives?

"Oh, Lillie," I said.

"May I remind you," she said, "that you are married to Bert?"

I sank my head into the couch pillow and closed my eyes.

"Barely."

"You're too tired now to know, but I remember that you and Bert were very much in love."

"We didn't do much about it." I opened my eyes and sat up. "Lillie, I don't even know where Bert is."

"He's here."

"He's in town?"

"He's very angry at you, dear."

"You saw him?"

"He was sitting right where you are on the couch this morning."

"Lillie," I said, "he didn't come up once to see me in Boston."

"He said you didn't want him."

"Well," I said helplessly, "Max was there, you see. Bert so despises him."

"He certainly does."

"And did he tell you I wanted to come home and he turned me down?"

"Well, that's when I scolded him," she said. "He was cruel to you, and I told him so."

"The marriage is over," I said. "He despises me, too."

Lillie was Hollywood royalty, and life's dramas to her were what the good earth is to the farmer. She leaned toward me.

"Dotty," she said omnisciently, "I have the feeling if you really wanted it, you could be as married to Bert as you might wish. Do you wish it?"

I sighed from a shallow part of me that seemed to have replaced feeling. "Lillie," I said wearily, "I don't think I wish anything."

"Dear Dotty," she said knowingly, "you will."

I got a flash that Lillie knew things I didn't. So did Anna. Others were alluding to an event that was breaking up the congestion in my life.

As I straggled up Fifth Avenue in the October twilight, the picture began to emerge. Bert had been to see Lillie; she and Anna were telling me I was going to have a new life. Somewhere in that walk through crowds, my steps quickened and an idea began to spread through me like Max's heat. It didn't seem loopy then.

I was supposed to marry Max.

By the time I reached Bonwit Teller I was obsessed with the idea: There was a master plan. Max was guiding society toward the good, and my place was to be grandly by his side in some queen capacity. The plan had shaped my whole life up to this climactic, imminent, solemn, celebratory moment, when I would become Max's bride. This was no vision; this was real.

Bert and I were through; I wasn't going to live with him anymore; the Hotel 14 would be our last home.

With terrible energy, I went through the door at Bonwit's and, using a check from our joint account, bought three beautiful robes, in which I would preside over Max's all-night gatherings of our family of patients. I would be quietly at the center, somewhere beyond love and happiness. Fate.

The saleswoman handed me my big box and said, "Do you want to sit down for a minute?"

"No, I'm fine, thank you."

"Well," she said, "enjoy wearing them."

She knew, too.

There were signs on the streets. As I walked up Madison Avenue in the dark, I saw some Con Ed men digging in a hole, with lights and poles with white streamers on them, fluttering in the breeze in celebration. Other signs in traffic: A driver giving way to me seemed to nod his head at my regal passage. A man tipped his hat at me and smiled.

I remembered that I owed Teddy a long run in the park.

When we came back, I lay down on the bed with him in my arms to wait.

The phone soon rang.

"Sweetie?" Bert sounded far away. "I've been trying and trying to reach you." His tenor voice cracked, and he sobbed. "I've been very cruel to you, cruel to you."

My hatred vanished.

"That's all right, darling, that's all right, don't cry, please don't," I said tenderly, altogether forgetting how cruel I'd been to him and was planning to be. I wanted to touch him, to kiss him deeply at this time of giving up, but my vision was still there.

"I guess I'll marry Max," I said, able to say the words now.

There was silence on the line.

"Where are you, Bertie?"

He cleared his throat. "At the Fifth Avenue Hotel." He had moved out and returned to his old bachelor neighborhood, Greenwich Village. I had to accept it.

"Aren't you going to come home?"

"I can't tonight." His voice was distressed, but his answer was final.

I took it as an instruction. I felt even more that I didn't have to make a decision; it was already made.

The next morning outside Max's office was double-parked the biggest, most serious-looking Rolls-Royce I had ever seen. It gleamed black in the sunlight, with great high fenders swooping downward and disappearing into the body. A man in a business suit sat at the wheel instead of a chauffeur.

The trees on the street were orange and yellow. Out of the doctor's ground-floor door came a scrawny, nervous, shuffling, unshaven man in a dark blue suit, his shirt open at the neck. He headed into the sunlight like an inhabitant of the night world exhibit at the zoo and climbed into the front seat. Some sort of underling, I thought.

There were people in the waiting room. The tough, florid intruder I had seen the day before was sitting at the desk.

I went up to her smiling. I still had the remnants of a talent for the friendly approach. It was my aim to charm this person into a smile that would acknowledge my rightful standing in this strange new office.

"Hello," I said engagingly, "I'm Mr. Alan Jay Lerner's assistant."

The woman nodded.

I stood my ground by the desk, waiting to be announced, but the woman picked up a magazine.

With another smile, I said, "We haven't met. What is your name?"

"Mrs. O'Connell," came the reply, but only barely.

Where was Beatrice, I wondered, the soft-spoken, fashionable European secretary who maintained classiness behind the desk?

"How do you like working for the doctor?"

"Who, Max?"

I felt a pang of distaste, almost alarm hearing this large Irish stranger calling the doctor Max. Who was she? Where did she come from? What was her connection to Max? She called him Max with no visible respect. Did she get his shots? As I stood asking questions of the air, the woman said, "Why don't you sit down over there and wait?"

Rebuffed, confused, I went to the couch. I had never spent more than five minutes in this waiting room before being admitted.

The door to the interior opened, and out of the warm, thriving family heart of the doctor's office came a woman of fashion. Black, sleek, short hair, white skin, dark red lips, whose heavy-lidded eyes gave her a languorous look that belied her adroit, businesslike manner as she went to the pay phone on the wall and dialed. "Ms. Bennet calling," she said imperiously. "Messages?"

She wrote in a crowded book.

I had seen her picture in issues of *Vogue*. She modeled sable, Cadillac, the big stuff. She represented the worldly, the *fait accompli*, the frankly demanding woman of wealth, power, and greed, and she obviously believed all of it. I hated her.

She hung up and stopped at the desk.

"The doctor is going . . ." Her voice lowered so that nobody in the waiting room could hear the rest. She did that on purpose, I thought.

As the woman turned to reenter the beloved realm behind the door, the six people in the waiting room sat back in their seats again and retreated into their own anxieties. They looked to be the ordinary assortment of devotees; only I knew none of them.

Mrs. O'Connell looked more like a prison guard than a secretary. I felt the entire cast of characters had changed while we were in Boston. The talkative, cultivated, artistic group had given way to these churlish, taciturn, oddly menacing people. I was dying to see Max.

There was a buzz. The woman picked up. Nodded.

"Go in," she said to me.

I jumped up and went through the miraculous door.

It was newly quiet in the corridors. I knocked softly.

"Come."

He was sitting at his counter, mixing. But he no longer sported tennis sneakers and polo shirt. In a black suit, white shirt, and black tie, he looked as if he were going to a funeral. He didn't look up at me.

Lying luxuriantly on the treatment table, elbow supporting her head, was the model, eyeing me with a slightly nasty smile. Two men I had never seen before were standing in the corner, watching. I knew only Mark Shaw, who stood behind Max in a guarding attitude. Mark looked at me in an unfriendly way. A small, blond, wizened man who rarely smiled, he was the White House photographer who had introduced Max to President Kennedy. He would one day die of a self-inflicted overdose of Max's medication. He was one of the few Max gave the privilege of giving themselves their own shots if Max were absent.

There was something disreputable about the group. I expected to see Peter Lorre pop out of the woodwork. I was obviously interrupting something.

"Some people are spreading it about," said the model to Max slowly, eyeing me with a bitter little smile, "that you're giving us all drugs."

"Oh, people are always ready to say that," I said quickly, "but it's just puritan ignorance."

The doctor made a sign for me to be quiet.

"Okay, hold out your arm, we don't have all day," he said in a low, thick voice. He still didn't look at me. Something sinister hung over him, and at the same time the tragic air of victim. The Holocaust. The concentration camp that he had escaped going to by a twist of fate at the Berlin airport.

He looked at me now through his thick lenses. I looked back, pouring myself out like water, but my look bounced off his opaque, hugely staring eyes. I was convinced that I was in danger and that these people were trying to take over and hold him hostage.

He put a needle in. I waited for heat, the heat of the calcium that rivaled the orgasm. But it didn't come. He wasn't giving me the real thing. I was unbelievably disappointed.

"I warned you about the eating," he said heavily. "You betrayed me. Whatever you do, don't go to the hospital. They kill people in the hospital."

What was he up to? I decided his words were a feint to get me safely out of there. This was some unexpected interruption of the master plan. That was the only explanation I could think of.

You can sometimes detect the approach of violence. I heard a rumbling, like the start of an earthquake, a scuffling, an alarmed, outraged exchange of voices, a physical something, almost tangible, charging the atmosphere with the thrust of opposing personalities. These sounds approached from behind the door. Suddenly it flew open with a crash, and there stood Bert Shapiro, a tiger, to whom I had once pledged my love and loyalty for the rest of my life. Rage contorted his face. Disgust. He strode up to Max, who was sitting on his stool, gave him a swift punch in the face, called him a dirty son of a bitch Nazi, grabbed me by the hand, and pulled me out through the waiting room and into his car, which was double-parked.

We drove silently over the Fifty-ninth Street Bridge, surrounded by steel girders and trucks, then onto the cobblestone
industrial streets with factories in Long Island City.

Eventually we made a turn onto the expressway, and things
got better. We put on some speed. Trees and grass appeared.
The road smoothened. At a suburb we exited and turned onto
a street with houses out of an advertisement for Cadillacs and
pulled up to one.

Dr. Barnett's office had a private entrance into the house. I
hadn't seen him since Bert and I got married. He had grown
a mustache.

"You're too thin," he said. I, who was always trying to shed
three pounds.

"That's what everybody says." I sighed, dropping into the
leather couch. "I thought I looked good."

"You don't." Obviously Bert and he had talked together
because he now said to me, as if surveying damages, "I've told
you, Doris," just as if we had gone on seeing each other, "you
live too much on the peaks—too much outside of your own
life."

Then why hadn't he cured me?

"You need to be detoxified. You have to go to the hospital
for a few days and get the poison out of you."

I didn't know how this would fit into the master plan, but
I was tired.

Dimly I realized this meant I would miss Alan's opening. It
was a relief.

Bert drove me directly to the big hospital, without stopping
to pick up clothes.

"I'll bring them to you," he said.

The emergency room was crowded. One man had been hit
by a baseball bat and was mashed and bleeding around his eye.

We sat in the dismal surroundings, without a magazine to read. After a while I was called. A friendly young doctor showed me a seat in a cubicle. He asked me questions.

"Do you know what day this is?"

"Yes," I answered, and told him.

"Do you know who the mayor of this city is?"

Detoxified! Christ! I thought, I'm in a psychiatric hospital!

Nevertheless, I followed Bert into the hospital elevator, which was large enough to hold a stretcher, along with a crowd of others, and we went up in silence, holding hands loosely. The doors opened. We had to ring a bell and be let in by a nurse, who unlocked the inner door.

As we entered the psychiatric department, standing before us in the hallway was a smiling, red-cheeked young man with black curly hair, full in the face, but slim in the hips through his rumpled hospital bathrobe.

"Welcome," he said. If he had had a bunch of flowers in his hand, it couldn't have felt more invitational.

"I'm Jay," he said.

"I'm Doris," I said, "and this is Bert."

I saw it all now, and my doubts vanished. Max was behind this after all; he had sent me here to hide out while he did battle with his enemies, and Jay was planted there by him as a companion, to greet me and divert me while I waited.

He led us to a large recreation room of pink and green. A few people were sitting peaceably in vinyl chairs and couches, some in conversation.

I didn't know what these people had to do to get there, but they all looked okay to me and every bit as normal as I was. There didn't seem to be anything wrong with anybody, especially Jay, who was showing us into a big institutional kitchen with stainless steel refrigerators.

"There's pudding and soda in here anytime you want it."

The nurses didn't wear uniforms up here. They dressed in their regular clothes. One, with a bright blouse and blue mini-skirt, came toward us.

"I'm Pat," she said. There was something about the carriage of her head and shoulders.

"Are you a dancer?" I asked.

"Was," she said.

Bert couldn't handle my clothing situation. Ever since the gold lamé robe, he had never bought me anything to wear. It was a subject we didn't discuss. But now he had to go home and pack up and bring me a hospital wardrobe. I asked for my three new robes, which he would find hanging ready for another purpose at the front of the closet. He wrote down on his little folded paper that was jammed with reminders in blue ink in his close printing.

"The pink, the turquoise, and the white . . . thank you. . . . Cosmetics . . ." I enumerated. "Sorry," I said, thinking of him having to deal with folding and packing. It was a kind of intimacy we'd never had.

"That little tan leather overnight case with my mother's initials."

"See you soon," Bert said, stuffing the paper into his pants pocket and scowling with responsibility.

Pat, the nurse, showed me to my room. We left Jay sitting in front of the television set.

The two hospital beds were empty, one in the high position, which I shunned, and the other by the window, low. I looked longingly at it. It was *my* bed.

I was utterly exhausted and jittery and counted on Pat, the nurse, to bring me one of Max's shots that he would have arranged for.

She handed me some limp pieces of white cloth. "Why don't you put these on until your husband brings your clothes?" she said, drew curtains around the low bed, and left me.

I sat at the edge, waiting for the next thing to happen.

It didn't take long. A brisk large black lady in a pink sweater sailed in with a tiny white paper cup with three pills in it.

"This will help you to relax," she said cheerfully.

"I don't want to relax," I said, turning away.

"You should take them." She jiggled the little cup in front of me.

"No, thank you."

"If you won't take them, we'll have to hold you down and give you a shot," she said calmly.

Well, a shot is what I had wanted in the first place.

"You need to sleep," she said with a hint of detached pity.

Just then a vase of bright yellow roses appeared in the doorway.

"For Doris Shapiro," said an attendant in white from behind the flowers.

The card read, "Hang on. Sleep and eat. Alan."

I accepted the flowers as significant. I remembered a Texan with red hair, who came to Max's from time to time. He used to sing "The Yellow Rose of Texas." The attendant placed them on the windowsill in the late-afternoon sun. I was sure the note from Alan was a message from Max. I would soon be rescued.

I gladly took the little paper cup now from the nurse, turned it upside down in my hand, and swallowed the three pills with one gulp of the water that she offered me.

I began to undress peacefully behind the curtains, and once in the limp hospital gown, with bare feet, I hung my clothes up in the narrow tin closet. I was already feeling sleepy and went for the bed.

Sleep is one of the most beautiful experiences in life. I had forgotten.

I slept as long as they would let me. A nurse prodded me

loose. Everybody had to get out of bed in the morning.

My clothes from Bert lay at the foot of the bed, and on the table beside me all the other things I had asked for, with a note in his angular handwriting: "Darling. Sleep. I'll see you tomorrow." Signed "B."

My yellow roses from Alan were basking in the morning sunlight on the windowsill. Nothing terrible had happened to me. I was still going to be queen.

I sat up. Slowly, in a state of bliss, I gathered my new turquoise robe, the cosmetics, and cleansing cream and scuttled down the corridor like a fugitive, to find the bathroom. To my relief, it was unoccupied. I locked the door of the tiled room.

First I rid myself of the horrid hospital clothing; then I stood for a long time under the hot, soothing shower, and, with no one trying to get in, I stroked makeup on my face in the mirror, fussed with my hair, and finally donned my robe.

I appeared at breakfast in the grandest robe in the hospital. And there were two more waiting, which I had hung up in the closet on wire hangers.

"You'll stop all of that in a day or so," said a wan woman patient in a short cotton housecoat, with slippers on bare feet.

"Not I," I said. "I would never appear without makeup."

Jay leaned toward me at the breakfast table, with a recreations director smile, and said, "After breakfast I'll take you up to the gym."

"First I have to make a phone call," I said. I had a few dimes in my bag and had taken note of the telephone booth in the recreation-dining room. I closed the door, which gave instant privacy, and sat on the little seat and dialed Max. Got the bad Mrs. O'Connell again. She wouldn't let me speak to him. Told me to call back. All right, I thought, I'm supposed to wait. From the window of the stifling booth, I saw Jay strolling back and forth in his pajamas.

We went up in the elevator. When the doors opened, we

were suddenly in a gym. Two fellows were dribbling a ball and shooting at a basket in their slippers. Jay went to the Ping-Pong table. I followed. If it weren't for the rumpled, washed-out hospital robes, I might have thought I was in a YMCA or YWCA.

We played. He was reckless and graceful with the racket, swinging from far back from the table. I was carefree and easy and hit some good balls, but once we started playing for points, there was no fight in me. After the first two or three losses, I didn't care and gave in to his pressure and got farther and farther behind.

In the afternoon, after lunch, I was summoned and went in my robe and sat around a large oval table with six or eight doctors, who wore shirts or suits—no white coats. They were a mixed group of men, very polite, didn't say much, but listened to me with great interest. I let them into my world easily. I thought: I'm already playing my role by introducing these inductees to Max's mysteries. They were initiates of the master plan for the good.

A slim, agile-looking doctor with rimless glasses and tight skin said, "What do you think it was Dr. Jacobsen was giving you?"

"Max knows more about enzymes than anyone else. He treated President Kennedy."

"What else do you think was in the shots?"

"Oh, I know," I said. And I told them, calling on all my powers to rhapsodize. They seemed riveted and didn't interrupt. Finally I said, "It is no secret. The secret is how he knows to combine all these things. Only a few people really understand what Max is doing."

A bald doctor with a double chin, who looked as though he hadn't been outdoors for ages, asked me, "Do you think he ever did you any harm?"

"Oh, never." I smiled at the group around the table. "And

you see, they're not habit-forming, because I'm here, perfectly fine, without a shot." That was my ace in the hole, my ultimate tribute to Max. I left the meeting feeling expansive. I took the pills that the nurses offered without protest now.

Bert came that night, and every other night. I waited for his footsteps. I loved him, you see. In a few days Alan's yellow roses faded and were replaced by Bert's brighter, hardier daisies, which were my favorite flowers anyway. They would last for my whole stay in the hospital.

One evening about a week later, Bert came in, kissed me lightly, and handed me the reviews of *On a Clear Day You Can See Forever.*

"You didn't miss much," he said.

I didn't devour them but read with the passing interest you might give to a stranger's obituary. The show took a beating; they praised the score. Barbara Harris was a star; John Cullum had a nice voice.

I was more interested in the quiet conversation Bert was having with Jay. We were sitting together in the lounge at visiting time. Jay, with his rosy face and black curly hair, was boyish; Bert could almost be his father.

"I was in Israel, too. How long were you there?"

"Three months. That's how I landed here in the hospital."

Bert, too polite to press, fooled with a rubber band, until Jay good-naturedly went on.

"I went over to be in the army," he said. "They put me in charge of a platoon. One night we were attacked, and I just cracked up. It was too much responsibility." He smiled.

He didn't seem to be cracked up to me.

Bert said, "How old are you?"

"Twenty-one."

Even though Jay was pals with Bert, he flirted with me. One day he put his arm around me, and I could feel the warmth through his bathrobe sleeve.

"You're the kind of woman a man could really get attached to," he said.

Woman! Nobody had ever called me anything but a girl before.

Worse, that night, after visiting hours, he crept to my bedside, took my hand, and whispered, "I've always wanted to have an affair with an older woman."

Impertinence. Never you mind, I thought, with your sneaky little affair in a hospital. My future is too grand for you to grasp.

Word must have gotten out that I was in the hospital, because in the next few days, unexpected guests from different times of my life came to see me at visiting hours. Life got to be rather social. A cousin appeared one evening whom I didn't usually socialize with. He brought me cookies. My old friend Marge, whom I hadn't seen in years, popped up at my bedside with a friend and a book called something like *Join the Club*. I could have questioned how she knew I was there as she didn't know Bert, but I didn't. I was sure *Join the Club* bore a hidden message from Max, which I would look for after everyone left. My two dear old aunts came during daytime visiting hours and told me, "You'll be all right."

So I was receiving, feeling at times almost gay. Everybody was telling me to be patient. Bert said, "You'll be out of here in a week or so." I noticed he didn't say I'd be *home* in a week or so.

Meanwhile, every day I would visit alone with young, red-bearded Dr. Rossner, who would politely ask a few questions. I couldn't see the point of those soft-toned meetings. They were like stray encounters of no consequence. I looked for messages from Max but decided Dr. Rossner was only a minor figure, playing a temporary holding role.

One morning I actually reached Max from the telephone booth. Gruff, almost silent, infinitely weighty and familiar, his voice carried his breath across the city blocks between us.

"When are you coming to see me?" I asked.

"No," he said. "Stay where you are. You'll be all right."

He talked to me as if there were people with him in the room. He was still under pressure. In danger perhaps. Even so, the reality of his voice revitalized me and lingered on in my ears as I went to the daily meeting of patients. But not for long. Something was beginning to chip away at my elation.

We sat in a semicircle, six or eight patients, with a moderator facing us in the middle. It was almost like a reading for one of Alan's shows. I was wearing my pink robe. Except for some hospital clothes, it could have been a gathering for the selection of a jury.

I had not a thing to say. I didn't listen either. It was a group therapy session. Jay suddenly burst into sobs and poured his heart out over an Israeli soldier whose death he felt he caused. Someone changed the subject immediately to something about herself. Impatient, my mind wandered over the past ten days or so. I had endured this waiting, the boredom, shuffling around in slippers in the corridors on linoleum floors, uninterested in the other patients, sustained in a limbo of waning expectancy. I slept hungrily, visited the doctors, played Ping-Pong, took pills, ate custard from the big refrigerator. I still didn't ask a question, because I didn't want an answer.

The whining now of the lady's voice from this group-therapy session, malingering in the artificial air in the curtained recreation room, with the suffocating smell of hospital food left over on trays, was beginning to creep upon me with a sense of incipient dread.

Out in the hallway a group approached. I saw a haunt of a man in a wheelchair, with the unmistakable ravaged look of cancer that I had seen on my mother two days before she died.

Dried blood stained the bandages on both his wrists, a testament to his last act of will, an attempt at suicide, an act that had obviously landed him, dying, in the psychiatric ward.

A big nurse, black, kind in the breezy way common to those private angels of the tormented, said to the victim, "We'll get you some lunch."

The man was beyond eating.

By his side, stepping as though on hot coals, was a distraught wife, with a faint, heartbreakingly amorous tilt to her head toward the ruin of the man.

They were treating death here!

As I pulled the sash on my pink robe tighter around my waist, I suddenly got a tragic intuition from my private world. Max was dying. The truth blazed in me. Max was dying. I had heard it in his voice that morning. I sat in the group, letting the feelings of loss flow through me like warm molasses.

Certainly that answered so many questions. Why I was being bivouacked here. Why they were reluctant to let me speak to Max. Why he had stopped giving me my shots in the first place. I may have spoken to him for the last time. That's why the doctors were listening to me with sympathy. That's why people I didn't usually see were coming to visit me. That's why Bert was forgiving me. Max was dying. I would never have one of his shots again.

I don't know how thought processes work, or if other people have dramas going on in their heads in the midst of doing other things, but as I gave myself to this grief, following its emerging images, like a spectator, a new vision took hold of me—not so tragic, but more awesome still.

Max wasn't dying. I was.

I felt a gush of pity for Bert. He was protecting me. They weren't telling me. Like my mother; we never told her she was dying. I made up my mind that I would pretend, as she did. I wouldn't tell Bert I knew. I would spare him. I wouldn't tell Max. I wouldn't burden anybody by telling I knew. My mother had taught me how to die. I wondered how it would come about. I didn't think I would die so young.

"How do you feel today?" said Dr. Rossner that afternoon. Why do so many young red-haired men wear beards? I thought. With blue eyes, too. We were sitting in a small room in the hospital with no window and a metal desk.

"Fine, thank you," I said.

"You look depressed," he said.

"I do?"

I don't remember what he answered or said for the rest of the visit, but with these three words, said in his soft-spoken voice, at the exact right time, like a surgeon with a knife, he excised my fantasies and severed me from them forever. In that quiet face-to-face conversation, he slid open the doorway, and I fell into the abyss of depression.

There would be no rescue, no messages from Max. Nobody was dying. There would be no transcending event. No events at all. My life was stripped bare of all subject matter.

What was going to happen was . . . nothing.

I was detoxified.

They sent me home a few days later, only about two weeks after the day Bert had stormed into Dr. Max's office and pulled me out.

The crisis was over. It seemed I had already withdrawn from Methedrine by merely agreeing to sleep again and take pills. There were to be no screaming bodily agonies, except, except this depression.

The dictionary defines "depression" as "a psychoneurotic or psychotic disorder marked esp. by sadness, inactivity, difficulty in thinking and concentration . . . feelings of dejection . . . a reduction in force . . . a lowering of vitality or functional activity." Add "terror," and I had it all.

Nevertheless, there was a destination every day, a gleaming moment of ecstasy awaiting me at nightfall: sleep. The price was the grief of waking up fifteen hours later at one in the afternoon, Bert long gone to work.

And the terror was the moment in the park when I unsnapped Teddy's leash, and with a little shake he ran joyously off around the lake. At a distance he would stop and look back at his ailing mother.

"Don't run away, darling," I pleaded with him. "Please don't run away."

In between, every trip to the stove to make a cup of coffee, or voyage to the bath, or worse, once a week outdoors, down the endlessly long half-block step by step to Madison Avenue and into a cab to go to talk to the therapist who had been assigned to me, Dr. Norman Decker, required the heroic will of a one-hundred-year-old woman.

Bert was being quietly my best friend. He was forever optimistic. On a bleak January 1 morning, he said to me, "Now spring is coming," and I said, "Now we're in for a long winter."

When Bert went to Ireland, a month later, Dr. Decker said, "I thought of sending you back to the hospital, but I think you can make it on your own. I'll see you twice a week instead."

I wrote to Bert. He answered, "Don't worry about being self-reliant, sweetie. You will be. We'll do all the wonderful things in the world together."

In those lonesome weeks of Bert's absence, my only company Teddy and that of Dr. Decker, I was not tempted to seek out Max. Even he and his shots couldn't fill my emptiness. He had receded in my thoughts. I didn't realize it then, but later knew that I was experiencing the breakup of my obsession. My cannibalism of genius, or talent, first of Alan, then of Max, was abating. It was a period of mourning.

Finally Bert wrote: "Wait for me at the airport."

I felt my first thrill, and somehow got there.

And somehow months passed and it became early summer. One evening, when I was sleeping less and beginning to cook small meals on the burner, I was returning from a visit to the rather mild Dr. Decker. Warm, rainy weather. People were scurrying for shelter, but I walked to Madison Avenue, turning my face up to catch the rain, as if I were taking a sunbath. The cabs going uptown were all filled. I didn't care. I would take a bus. I hadn't been on a bus with other people for a long time. One came, crowded with late-afternoon travelers. I stepped up, wet, paid, and inched my way through the crowd to a place where I could hang on to a strap.

I looked around at the people standing on the bus. All strangers. They looked nice. A little weary. Going home. I was going home, too. Bert would come at six-thirty.

From within the crowd something flashed past my mind's eye. A familiar face. Too fleeting to grasp. I looked around. There was no one I knew. But there it was again. That image. There was someone on this bus I knew. Someone close. Infinitely close and loved. I looked into the crowd. Was Bert on this bus? My mother even? Closer. My own child? If I had one. I searched the crowd seriously now. Maybe I was hallucinating again. The face filled my heart, stopped my breath with tenderness. I seemed to be able to spot it now when I wanted to. Where? On the edge of the crowd. There. In the mirror. It was *my* face. It was a mirror I was seeing. It was my own face in the crowd in the mirror by the door that I had fallen in love with.

This sounds narcissistic, but if you haven't been on good terms with your face for a long time, finding that it's your nearest and dearest can be a sign you've recovered.

Passion returned to Bert and me that night, the ultimate celebration between a man and a woman. Primal energy surged. Married love began. I felt once more illuminated by the immense privilege of marriage—to Bert. I had been right the first time.

The only mention Bert ever made of the whole experience and his rescue of me was "Before you could be shaken loose from those people, your life had to be endangered."

I felt the awed relief of the lucky person. Again life's worst had only nipped me and turned to naught.

X

Alan didn't marry Frances Douglas. But they remained friends, and he probably went to her benefit parties for the American Indian.

He didn't marry Lisa Echols. Her parents came and took her back to California to a doctor, where she regained her health, married a musician, and had at least one child. For some years she flew back to New York to work with Alan for a few weeks here and there.

He didn't marry Susan Savage. She stayed on with him in some capacity for a few years and now argues in court on behalf of one of the networks.

I didn't see Alan for two years after the opening of *On a Clear Day You Can See Forever.*

One morning he called me in California, where Bert and I were spending the summer awaiting the birth of our daughter. I was seeing a lot of Lillie.

Alan's voice was as intimate as ever; he dazzled me all over again. Would I like to come over and see him? He was at the Beverly Hills Hotel.

I went. The surroundings reminded me of the first time I met him. Another elegant, discreet tropical bungalow, with hotel service. Karen Gundersson was with him. He was as friendly, even as gallant as when I had first known him.

"I want to read you *Coco.*" His new show.

I sat down in one of those familiar deep chairs again, and he read the whole play. He had actually persuaded Katharine Hepburn to come out of retirement and star in her only musical, to play the great Coco Chanel, the dauntless French designer who freed women permanently by changing their dress and cutting off their locks. The composer was André Previn. It had all the marks of a Lerner hit. But I was miles away from being even faintly interested in being any part of it. I would never again take somebody else's passion for my own. I had Bert.

I clapped my hands when he came to the end. Then he looked up at me and said, without a hint of vanity, almost humbly, "I wrote it all myself." I'll never understand why Alan needed to tell me this, but I was touched to the quick at his offering me this prize.

Alan never had the luxury of keeping a sketchbook, say, like Cézanne. When he got an idea and spoke it, he was instantly plunged into a commitment of huge consequences—to many people and vast sums of money. In the young days he throve on this. But his manner of working had become more and more of a burden to him, as his romanticism was overtaken by the sixties and seventies, the sexual revolution through which, as Bud says, the romantic tension between a man and a woman evaporated, and in its place came Vietnam, flower children, and the appearance of such overproduced and underwritten works as *Jesus Christ Superstar, Cats, Starlight Express.*

It seems to me it's still as hard as it always was to write something really good, and—listen—just because many more people than ever are trying doesn't change the fact that only a rare few can or do, now as always. Alan Lerner was one of those few.

Do you remember a man for his best works or his last? His best, without a doubt. That's why Alan continued to receive honors up until the time of his death. His lyrics are as fresh, as elegant and subtle, as tantalizing today as when they were written. If he got confused or impulsive when picking a property in his changing world, well, he paid the price.

When he finished reading me *Coco*, he leaned forward and told me in the familiar way he liked to spring surprises, that tomorrow he and Karen were going to drive up to Santa Barbara and get married. We had champagne. We had lunch. I kissed them both. And that was the last time I ever saw him.

He had three more wives after Karen, making a total of eight, and wrote three more shows.

A few years later I picked up *The New York Times* one morning and saw Max Jacobson's familiar face on the front page. An enraged relative of a patient had turned the law on him. People were always threatening to do that. He was taken to court and in the end lost his license to practice medicine of any kind.

Max was not a simple charlatan. He was a far more complicated one, brilliant, mysterious in his power to manipulate and orchestrate all the body systems and the mental ones as well. He had about him a symptom of greatness.

But he was corrupt to the core.

So were we all. We wanted something for nothing: extra life, thrills, privilege. And we got it. Until some of us cracked up.

Alan escaped, but not until he went through his own hell. Bud paints a chilling picture, but only in outline. Because he never participated in that side of Alan's life, he doesn't know details, and doesn't want to.

It seems that Alan found another doctor, who sent him packages from Washington. Alan became adept at the needle; he gave himself his own injections of whatever the stuff was. Bud said, "After a while he was black and blue all over."

But after another while Alan weaned himself away and,

according to Bud, became free. I'm just glad I never got any packages from Washington.

A fall afternoon in 1988. A chance encounter as I walked up Third Avenue in the Seventies. A face coming toward me plunged the clock back twenty-three years, taking me with it.

"Beatrice!" I felt the soft contours of nostalgia shaping inside me. She was a fellow survivor.

Bravely maintained over a decade, in her New York elegance, with an understated flair that bespoke European origins, she seemed inclined to stop and chat.

For all the many times I had passed by her at the desk in the days at Max's office, she was a mystery. All I knew about her was that she had some vague Old World connection to Max and Nina. Now she was telling me she had been a dancer.

"Ah, yes," she said, in her German alto voice, "we were Gomez and Beatrice. We opened at the Rainbow Room, danced at the Copacabana, the Waldorf, all over."

That explained the sleek look.

"I had another partner before, but I didn't like him. Gomez was a lady-killer. He was gorgeous. The women were crazy about him. Only I knew he was a homosexual, so I didn't have any problems with him."

I dared broach the subject that lay tacitly between us.

"What did you think of Alan and me, coming and going day after day to see Max? Did you think we were nuts? Did you know we used to come all night, too, when you had gone home?"

She nodded elegiacally. I dared go farther.

"Did you ever take Max's shots, Beatrice?"

"I did. But I stopped. They left an ugly mark on my arm. And who wanted sleepless nights? I told him he could give me vitamins in the hip, but none of that Methedrine."

It amazed me. She simply never fell for it. Why did she stay?

I didn't want her to take flight. "What about Nina?" I asked carefully.

"Nina was grief-stricken that Max never wrote up his work. She begged him to, but he never would. At one point she didn't want his shots anymore."

I remembered vividly the night at the Waldorf offices about a week before her death when Nina allowed him to coax her into the other room.

"How did you meet Max?"

"Oh, when we left Germany, I lived with my parents in the same apartment house in Paris as Max and Nina did. Nina was my best friend."

We stood silently. She didn't move to leave. I asked, "Is it true that Max flew every week to the White House to treat President Kennedy?"

"No, not every week. But he went numerous times. And poor Max, he was hurt because they always showed him through the back door."

I took a deep, careful breath. "Beatrice," I said, "what happened to Nina?"

She looked into my eyes. With a crestfallen face, very softly she said, "I'm afraid Max did it."

I had always known it.

We stood, dodging shoppers and delivery carts in front of the market on Third Avenue, as her words softly landed in the air between us, closing the gap of twenty-three years.

"What did the hospital say she died of?"

"Oh, they said some virus or something, I don't know."

"How come there was no autopsy?"

She raised her hands in bewilderment. "Nobody ever asked for one."

Only two more questions: "What about Alan? Did he stick to Max when he was in trouble?"

"He tried to get Louis Nizer to defend Max, but Nizer passed it on to one of his lesser lawyers, and Alan faded away. It was a terrible day when he had to take his license off the wall. I was there. He died trying to get it back."

On August 3, 1977, I ran into Fritz Loewe. I know the date because it was the morning after the night my brother, Howard, died. This time life's worst had caught up with me. It was the real and chilling thing. Cancer.

It was Santa Barbara. I stopped for gas at a station that looked like a resort. Up drove a big convertible, top down, a young blond female at the wheel, and out of it stepped Fritz.

"I'm seventy-five," he said smugly, glancing at the blonde in the car.

"My brother died last night," I said.

"Oh, that's terrible. I don't want to hear about it."

At seventy-five, I didn't blame him.

"Why don't you come see me?" he said. "I'm here for the summer."

I would have loved that, but not then. He lived eleven more years, but I never saw him again.

A couple of years ago I watched Lerner and Loewe on television at the Kennedy Center, receiving the Presidential Award for lifetime achievement. Fritz looked like an ancient, fragile version of himself. But aside from the squarish shape of his head and jaw and his tuxedo, Alan was hardly recognizable. He was dying. Cancer.

He died a few months after, in June 1986. At the time I read the news, Bert, too, was dying, and did so five months later in the first few minutes of November 1, 1986. Cancer. Alan was sixty-eight and Bert was sixty-six.

I've seen Bud. He remained Alan's best friend and collaborator through all the years and was with Alan and his family a few hours before his death. He says, "I liked all of Alan's wives; they were wonderful girls."

Sometimes I can see Alan lounging in a deep chair, feet in white moccasins, puzzling over some words. "Sit back, read the newspaper. I'll have something for you in a minute."

And I can hear Bert say to me, "Sweetie, it's so easy to not do something."

So I wrote this book.

INDEX